GRIT n' GRACE

GRIT
n'
GRACE

BY
NORMA HENDRIX-BRUNSON

A WOMAN'S JOURNEY TOWARDS EMBRACING
LIFE'S DEFINING MOMENTS

XULON PRESS

Xulon Press
2301 Lucien Way #415
Maitland, FL 32751
407.339.4217
www.xulonpress.com

Unless otherwise indicated, Scripture quotations taken from the Holy Bible, New International Version (NIV). Copyright © 1973, 1978, 1984, 2011 by Biblica, Inc.™. Used by permission. All rights reserved.

Paperback ISBN-13: 978-1-6628-4401-0
Ebook ISBN-13: 978-1-6628-4402-7

With deep gratitude
I dedicate this book

To
My parents
Spurgeon and Fae Hendrix
For teaching me The Way.

To
My Husband
Robert Worth Brunson
For walking with me on The Way.

To
My daughters
Robin and Sheri
For blessing me on The Way.

To
My Spiritual Guide
Dr. Larry Fine
For encouraging me on The Way.

Table of Contents

PREFACE

BURIAL, NOVEMBER 9, 2018

I just laid my best friend in a gaping hole. Husband of 54 years, partner in ministry, father and grandfather, a gifted artist, and a faithful follower of Jesus Christ. As I dropped rose petals in that black abyss, I spoke tearfully and gratefully,

"Thank you, Bob Brunson, for choosing me. Thank you for all we learned together, for the places we have been, and the wild ride God has seen us through. The Way has not always been smooth, but we held steady and together through it all. I will always love you. I can't wait to see you again!" I told the shovel man to go ahead. I waited until the hole was no more. I wept.

It was not the first gaping hole I had spoken into.

CHAPTER I

BROKEN SPIRIT

I signed myself into the Lutheran Medical Center Psyche Unit on December 12, 1982, at 11:00 pm. I told Bob and the girls good-bye and followed the night nurse into a room. I was exhausted. I slipped into a gown and threw myself under the covers. I did not care. I wanted to sleep and never wake up.

The next morning came too early. I was taken to the dining room for breakfast and then orientation. I soon became acquainted with my roommate, a beautiful 18-year-old brunette. She said she did not want to live, but knew she needed help. Here I was, next to her, desiring the same. The only difference between us besides our age, was that I donned a huge Bible next to my bed. The rest seemed similar; two human beings in need of help.

Two days after arrival I met the psychiatrist. He asked me about my life, my experiences, what was troubling me. I bared my soul with no reservations. He looked at me and said,

"You will take a battery of tests that will help us determine your best plan of care. Now tell me about yourself. Start wherever you want. I'm listening."

BACKGROUND

My father was born in a Stigler, Oklahoma, on November 20, 1911, to Edgar and Lillie Hendrix. He was the eldest of seven children. When my father graduated from Business School in Tulsa, Oklahoma, he began searching for work. One day, a neighbor by the name of Reese Pegan came by and asked my father a life changing question. "Spurgeon, what are you going to do with the rest of your life?" Spurgeon told him he did not know but was searching for a place of employment. Reese then asked, "Why don't you decide to attend Bethany Peniel College in Bethany, Oklahoma? I'll take you there and even help with some of your expenses." He packed up and headed for college.

During a chapel service, he gave his heart to the Lord and later, answered the call to preach. After he graduated, he held a tent meeting close to where his parents lived. It was then that his father and mother gave their hearts to the Lordship of Jesus Christ.

While in college, he met a beautiful, dark headed woman, by the name of Oma Fae [Higgins] Lytle. Fae was born in Ringwood, Oklahoma on March 25, 1909, to Alonzo and Emma Higgins. The Higgins had five living children. When Fae was three years old, Emma died of tuberculosis and

2

was buried at the Flat Rock, Indiana cemetery on July 11, 1912. Alonzo felt he could not care for all his children by himself. Little Fae was adopted by Marion and Sylvia Lytle. Ruby, 13 went to live with Alonzo's sister and Alonzo cared for the boys, Ebert, Raymond, and Virgil.

Fae's new home was back in Ringwood with the Lytles Their farm rested on the banks of the Cimarron River. They had been married 18 years when they adopted Oma Fae. Fae recalls that her life was difficult. Sylvia was an intense, complicated and a disturbed woman. Fae recounts the countless times when Sylvia screamed in distress, "The Devil is about to get me!"

One night, when Fae was about seven years old, Sylvia came into her room with a lantern and a gun. She pointed the gun at Fae's head, "Your doom is sealed!" Fae remembers numerous incidents of abuse, neglect, shame, and fear. As her daughter, I saw evidence of the mistreatment my mother suffered. She was intense, many times nervous, even as she led a life of prayer and service to God and others.

My mother graduated from Central State Teachers' College in Edmond, Oklahoma, and taught school. During those days, she was dating my father. Sylvia never accepted him for she wanted another man to be her son-in-law. One day Sylvia blurted out, "I may be going to hell, but Spurgeon Hendrix will be there when I get there." She and my father were married June 2, 1935, in Bethany, Oklahoma. Marion and Sylvia disinherited her.

3

Fae says that what held her together was her real encounter with God. One day she surrendered her life and felt a definite call to serve God as a missionary. My father had the same call.

They became pastors in Indiana. In 1941 they were assigned as missionaries to Argentina by the General Board of the Church of the Nazarene. One August day that year, they boarded a ship and sailed from the New York harbor.

CHAPTER II

BUENOS AIRES, ARGENTINA

*I*t was on a cold August 12th day in 1943, that I was delivered by C-Section at the British Hospital, in Buenos Aires. Fae Hendrix said she "wanted a sweet baby girl and prayed for one." Well, she got the baby girl. As to the sweet, time would tell. Brother Ray was disappointed that the "baby couldn't play soccer."

The Bering Iglesia del Nazareno church ladies knitted sweaters, blankets, dresses, caps, and booties. Baby Norma Luisa had all the clothes she needed. I keep some of those baby clothes in my cedar chest to remember their kindness.

Spurgeon was proud of me; a girl who would bear his facial features as well as aspects of his temperament and personality. His first duty was to register me at the American Embassy in Buenos Aires. Being born in Argentina, of American parents, gave me dual citizenship. When I turned 18, I chose to be an American Citizen. However, in Argentina, I am still considered Argentine and just recently activated my Argentine citizenship. Someone asked me, "Why?" I answered, "Just because I can!"

My earliest recollection at the age of two is vivid. While I slept in a baby crib, I kept hearing a noise during the night. My imagination told me that someone was trying to get in through the roof. I later discovered it was my father's loud snore in the next room. I was not afraid, simply curious. I felt safe, special, and loved.

BOUND FOR THE USA

My next memory is at the age of three, when my mother told me that we were going on a trip, and I needed to leave my favorite doll for a while. So, she led me to the cedar chest, and we knelt. She took my doll in her hands and talked to her as if she were alive.

"Now dolly, your mommy is going to be away for a while, so we are going to wrap you up real tight and let you sleep while we are gone."

I still remember the feeling of safety about leaving my doll asleep in the cedar chest. My mother knew me well and wisely handled what might have otherwise been an unnecessary bout of tears and distress.

The sense of wellbeing evaporated quickly. The plane ride to the United States was rough. It was the first time I remember feeling fear. I saw flashes of green and blue lightning. Loud thunderclaps! The plane jumped around like a broken toy. Meanwhile, my mother was crying and praying out loud! I wanted her to be calm, but she was not. I wanted to help her, and I could not. My father was across the aisle with my brother. I do not remember how long the storm lasted. I disliked seeing my mother so out of control.

We settled in a small cottage in Indian Lake, Michigan. My mother, pregnant with my younger brother, was scheduled for a Cesarean. I was sent to live with a young couple. I was almost four. She and her husband lived in a big house. There were no children around.

For some reason, I did not feel comfortable with them. I felt they loved their dog more than they cared for me. I really missed my mother. I guess I spent about a month with them. My memory is sharp as I recall the loneliness and fear I felt.

I was still wearing a diaper at bedtime in case of a midnight mishap. One night, the woman laid me down to diaper me. The husband came and stood beside her looking down at me. I hated him looking at me while I was naked. This was the first time I remember feeling shame. And I felt afraid and unprotected.

After my mother recovered from her C-Section and the birth of my brother, Spurgeon Leon, we moved to Manchester, Indiana, while my father traveled to churches speaking about the church work in Argentina.

I started hearing these words, "She is so strong willed!" I must have misbehaved somehow, because I received a strong spanking one night when we returned from church. Following the whipping, I was sent to my room. After a while, my mother called me out and said, "Now honey, wouldn't it have been better if you had not misbehaved tonight?" Something inside of me stood up and I yelled, "NO!" Swift was the response in the form of a fly swatter across my behind. At the end I was contrite and said, "Yes, Mommy, I'm sorry!" I never said "No!" again to my mother until eight years later.

I had neighborhood friends. My mother seemed happy and joyful. I have pictures of my brother Ray and me sitting around the Christmas tree. I loved playing in the snow for the first time in my life. I still picture my mother rocking my baby brother and me as she sang, "There's a peace in my heart, that the world never gave. A peace it cannot take away." She sang until we fell asleep.

I picked up the same practice with my girls. My mother died at the age of 105 in 2014. Following the funeral, we returned to our hotel in Olathe, Kansas. As I was preparing for bed, Robin said, "Mom, do you know what you are humming? Mom, you are humming, 'There's a peace in my heart!'" I truthfully did not even think what I was humming. My mother must have been loudly singing from up yonder! That was a cherished, angel moment.

CHAPTER III

BACK HOME IN TERRERO 960

$\mathcal{W}$e returned to the same house on Terrero Street in Buenos Aires. My brother Ray and I shared a room. My father built a partition to give us each privacy. My brother Ray loved to listen to Tarzan on the Radio, and he built himself a "listening booth" out of one of our large crates. He placed a lamp, a radio, and an extension cord inside. When Tarzan came on, I knew I better leave him alone.

Even though we lived in the center of Buenos Aires, the property included a large back yard. I had pets of all kinds, dogs, birds, rabbits, cats. Ray built a tunnel in the back yard, and I remember how much fun it was to go into it. I called one tree "my horse" because the trunk was bent so that I could climb on it and pretend I was a "gaucha", riding the Argentine pampas.

One day some men came and dug several holes in the ground. I found out they were the posts for a large tent. For some reason, I wanted to know if the hole was deeper than my little brother, Leon was tall. So, I tried to stick him in the hole, but his arms, legs and screams got my mother's attention. She came out and put an end to my mathematical inquiry with the use a little switch across my legs and back end. I did not try that again.

Every year, at the same time, we heard a snipping sound in the middle of the night. My father called us out and with a flashlight showed us the row of ants walking in straight lines, carrying large leaves. One by one they stripped the tree bare in one night. It always amazed me!

My brother Ray decided to teach me how to box. That went well until he bloodied my nose. My mother put a stop to that.

I was six years old when I remember telling my first lie. I accidentally threw a rock in the wrong direction, and I broke a window. My mother came to me and asked, "Norma, do you know who broke that window?" I responded, "What window?" "The side window." I looked shocked and said, "No, I don't know."

Church was long and boring. The people all seemed old, and they prayed out loud forever! The ladies wore dark colors, with long sleeves, high necks, hair up in buns. The women sat on one side and the men on the other. The men old and serious, wore suits and ties. I remember thinking that either the men were afraid of the women or the women afraid of the men because their sure kept their distance! There were two other girls my age in church. Our Sunday School teacher was uninspiring. She read from a little sheet of printed material about things that I did not understand or care a whit about. But she droned on and on.

Sometimes the church board organized skits and dramas to tell Bible Stories. I loved being in plays. I was mischievous. One night while in church, I went to the bathroom. The bidet next to the toilet looked like a willing cohort. I turned the water on, and it spurt up to the ceiling. I left it running, walked out of the bathroom and closed the door. Yes, I did get a whipping! I guess I deserved that one!

BELIEVING

I was six years old, when one Sunday, I was brought face to face with the lie I held hidden in my heart. I do not remember the preacher or his message, but when he opened the altar for prayer, I knew I had to go. I ran to the altar, began crying and confessing my lie to Jesus and then later to my mother.

I have never gotten away from that moment of encounter when the Spirit of God wooed my heart to Himself. It was life changing. That night I believed Jesus forgave me. From then on, I lived a normal childhood, but always sensed a great desire to read the Bible and love Jesus. I thank God for parents that prayed for me and modeled the life of forgiveness and grace as I weathered the storms of teen, college years and beyond.

The psychiatrist was listening intently. When I shared this part of my life journey, I sensed he was clueless about this "fluttering, emotional, spiritual event" on which I had placed so much emphasis in sharing my life story. He almost interrupted me, but did say, "Go on, I'm listening." Throughout this extended "story of my life" he kept asking, "What were you feeling? Can you see any pattens in your behavior?"

BUENOS AIRES AND SCHOOL

My brother Ray and I traveled across the city of Buenos Aires to attend school at Ward and Lincoln Schools. School in Argentina was full-time, Spanish in the morning and British School system in the afternoon and on Saturday mornings. Pencils were non-existent for us. We began writing with ink pens in the first grade. We carried our own ink bottles to refill our pens when needed. We learned to write cursive from the beginning and to this day, printing is more difficult for me than cursive.

I was terrified my first day of school. My mother left me at the classroom door after hugging me goodbye. I was surrounded by total strangers. I had been with strangers before, and I didn't like that feeling. I made it though. Little by little I began to relax and understand that no one was going to hurt me. My brother Ray, who was six years older than I, waited for me after school. It took an hour for the bus ride home.

One day as we rode to school, my lunch pail accidently opened, and my sandwich and orange got trampled on the ground. My brother was embarrassed and angry. He yelled at me all the way home.

On another bus ride, I desperately needed to go to the bathroom. Suddenly he noticed a trickle of humidity running down towards the front of the bus. He was furious! He got off many blocks earlier than our stop and left me alone on the bus. I was extremely afraid. I was six years old at the time and managed to get off at our stop. But brother Ray got a big whipping!

Recess was a time of playing on the trapeze, swings and instigating a game of "Cops and Robbers". I always wanted to be the cop. One day, I swung up to grab onto the trapeze bar but missed and hit the bar with my mouth, breaking my front tooth. I donned that broken tooth for a long time until finally securing a dentist willing to tackle the job of repairing it. Those were my tomboy days.

Once a year, churches in the United States boxed up gifts, clothes, and goodies for us. We loved getting gifts from the homeland. My brother Ray filled hours of fun with train he received. I watched Ray and my dad fix up his train track and I loved to hear the whistle and see the little headlight on as the little train puffed its way on the track.

I still have the little doll that I received. My grandmother sent some knitted and crocheted clothes for it, and I treasured that doll and my grandmother's kindness.

One of the gifts was a pair of rubber boots which I had to wear to school on rainy days. I hated them! No one wore boots! And no one took black lunch pails to work or school! I felt I stood out and everyone was staring at me.

On a rainy, "boots to school day", the teacher announced that the person who behaved the best would have the privilege of holding the Argentine flag during the assembly. I determined right there and then, to set about performing a series of mischievous acts to bypass the honor of holding the blue and white Argentine flag while wearing my black, embarrassing American boots. There was a pattern brewing.

Mother took me weekly across town on the public bus to my piano lessons. My teacher was a strict single woman that to my five-year-old mind seemed to be 120 years old! And I knew why she was not married. The woman was mean! Her house smelled musty. She smelled crusty but could she play the piano! And she was determined I was going to learn to play as well.

I had one on her though... when a new piece was chosen, she first played it for me to show me the fortes, the pianos, the pianissimos, the rests on how to express the piece. Unknowingly, she helped me hear the piece, so I did not have to work so hard at reading music. I began relying more on the first-time hearing than on working on reading the sheet music. She never caught on. Had she not done that, I would have had to work harder at reading music and would have become more comfortable with it. My first recital took place when I was six, and every year after that until furlough.

The piano became my friend. I loved to sit and play hymns by ear, composing untold variations of "Creation", "When Jesus Arose", "Storms" and so many more. The piano and I belonged together. So many years later, I was able to play the 1812 Overture, just for fun and just because I could. Today I thank my mother for her investment in me.

The psychiatrist must have heard enough for one sitting. He told me we would continue tomorrow. He arranged for me to get onto the computer to begin taking tests. I answered hundreds of questions and was glad when that was over. The next morning, I was sent to his office again. "Please continue," he said.

CHAPTER IV

BOAT RIDE ON THE SS BRAZIL

*M*y parents were scheduled for their second furlough. The exciting day arrived to board the SS Brazil; the large ship owed by the Moore McCormick lines. We spent 17 days at sea. I was 12.

The ship was huge, and our cabin was small. But it was an adventure. The ship organized a Costume Party and my brother Leon, and I dressed up in made-up costumes. I won a bracelet and to my shock, my mother allowed me to wear it! Another first was our going to the theatre on board and watching the movie, Heidi. I was star-struck.

One morning we awoke to find the staff handing out small hand-held flags of the United States. They said, "We are nearing Ellis Island and will soon dock." My family and I stood on deck with many other passengers and began waving flags as we sailed past the Statue of Liberty. My heart swelled as we began to hear a band playing the "Star Spangled Banner" "America the Beautiful" and others. I was deeply moved and never forgot that moment of pride in being an American.

BONDING WITH EXTENDED FAMILY

Family reunion with the Hendrix clan marked a bonding that stands to this day. We met in Coban, Oklahoma at my grandparents' home. My cousins and I rode our grandfather's truck as he made rounds in the oil fields, checking pumping stations, and water vats. We romped and played hide and seek, climbed trees, and became family friends.

We drove to Indianapolis to visit Aunt Ruby and family. Aunt Ruby was my mother's only living sibling. I enjoyed her large, three-story home on Tibbs Avenue. I also remember that we must have been there Memorial Day because we could hear the roar of cars at the Speedway.

I did not like one member of Ruby's household. He invited me to sit by him and he put his hands on my breasts. I felt uneasy and I finally got up. I did not tell my mother. I was afraid. And I kept my distance. He never bothered me again.

A pastor in Indianapolis asked my mother if I would like to attend girls' camp, and my parents consented. I boarded a Greyhound bus to a small drop-off point somewhere in Indiana. A kind pastor picked me up and drove me to camp. I found joy and friendship. I was also mischievous. One night, we found a mouse sitting under my bed. Somehow, I was able to pick up that mouse who consequently bit my thumb. We had to inform the camp leaders who immediately rushed me to an Emergency Room to check out my bite. I know they were thrilled with me!

One night around a campfire, during a full moon, I felt God's call upon my life. It went something like this, "Norma, that full moon is a mirror, reflecting the other side of the world. Would you go anywhere I ask you and tell them about Me?" My immediate response was "Yes Lord" and the tears began to flow. My call to help lead others to Him began that night. And it has never left me. I was honored to be voted Camp Queen! That felt good!

BARTLESVILLE, OKLAHOMA

We settled on Wyandotte street where I enrolled in 5th grade again. I had gone through half of the 5th grade since our school year in Argentina runs from March to November. I learned to play Tether Ball but have little recollection of that school year. What do I remember is that I had the mumps, I received and rode a new bicycle, plus collecting a pet harem; [dog, cat, bird, horny toad, fish, spiders], any animal held my rapt attention. I enjoyed watching Television at my friend Carolyn's house.

There were two things about my parents that I was sure about: They loved God first and they loved me and my brothers. I had no doubt. I loved them and felt secure in that fact. Now as an adult, I know that they, as I, made some mistakes that had unintended consequences.

"Let me ask you, why are you telling me this about your parents? It sounds to me like you are trying to convince me that they loved you. Is that so?"

Well, I didn't understand what was so strange about my comment and I thought it strange that he would ask me. I answered, "I don't know."

"Let me hear more."

I received the whipping' of my life in Bartlesville. Both my parents and I never forgot it and we both learned from it. My parents left for a few hours. I was told to wash the dishes. I said "Okay." They left. I forgot.

When they returned my mother said,

"Norma, you didn't wash the dishes."

"Oh, I'm sorry! I forgot!"

I saw my mother go outside and cut a switch. She came back to the bedroom and said,

"Norma, I want you to lie down and take your punishment."

Something welled up in me and I was bound and determined I would not lie down.

"NO!" I said. This was my second NO.

The whipping started. "Norma, lie down."

"NO!" She whipped and I jumped around. She called for my father. "Spurgeon, bring the belt."

My father came in and started swishing that belt around, hitting my legs. My legs were bleeding now. But I was not going to lie down. He got tired and my mother started in again. I cannot say exactly how long this standoff continued, but it was a long time. They took turns from belt to switch. But I was not going to take my punishment lying down.

I finally was so exhausted from jumping and avoiding the hits, that I collapsed exhausted, face down on the bed, crying. My parents fell on the bed beside me, crying. "Norma, why are you so stubborn?"

That was my last spanking.

He stopped me. "Tell me, are you still standing?"

I thought for a moment and then replied, "Yes, or I wouldn't have walked into this psyche ward."

He smiled. "Go on."

BELONGING

I never had the feeling of "Belonging" in Bartlesville, except when we visited my grandparents in Coban. My grandmother's love for me was so evident. When we arrived in the United States for furlough and I was three, my grandmother cried because she talked to me in English, and I answered in Spanish. I always felt she loved me in a special way.

BLUE MOUNTAIN RANGE, LA GRANDE, OREGON

In Argentina, my parents seemed to always be stressed, busy, worried, running, doing. I constantly sensed their tension. They both had major surgeries during that last term.

So, they were afforded two years of either deputation or pastoring.

During the second furlough year my parents took a pastorate in La Grande, Oregon, a cozy little town surrounded by the Blue Mountain Range. My father was home more. My mother was home all the time and she seemed really "present" for the first time in my life. We listened to radio programs together. It seemed my parents had "friends" that they palled around with.

I thoroughly enjoyed school. . . the sixth grade with Mr. Webb. I learned to hit a ball in softball. I had my first boyfriend, Dallas, and my mother allowed me to wear jeans. Wow was that ever a great year!

I learned more about prayer. While studying science in school, I discovered that white rats are used in laboratories for testing. One day I prayed, "Lord, I would love to have a white rat!" Lo and behold, my friend came to me two weeks later and said, "A lady has white rats, do you want one?" And sure enough I came into the possession of a white and black rat which I thoroughly enjoyed as my pet.

I continued with piano lessons and was happy that I could play my recital, ten-minute piece, "The Persian Market" by heart and without making a mistake. My parents were proud as well.

It was in La Grande Oregon that my mother taught me all about the process of procreation. I will never forget my reaction. YEUUhhhhh!! My mother laughed and said, "You won't always feel that way!" The year flew by, and we received the news that my parents were being sent to Cuba. I hated saying goodbye to my pets. But even more difficult was the saying goodbye to my brother, Ray, who was enrolled at Nampa Nazarene College in Nampa, Idaho.

The doctor stopped me. He reiterated the aspects that created my sense of belonging. We talked about that a while.

He alluded to my love of pets. He asked if I ever had close friends. I told him yes, a few, but mainly my pets and one or two friends. I told him about my "La Grande friend" who was the poorest girl in the neighborhood. No one wanted to be her friend. I told him that I felt sorry for her, so I became her friend. They lived in the poorest house in the neighborhood and even in their house, had a huge hole in the kitchen floor which they avoided all the time.

He asked me if I felt sorry for the girl or for myself. I did not understand. But I figured it didn't matter anyway. But then, perhaps it did!

He told me he would see me next session

CHAPTER V

BONGO DRUM PARADISE, HAVANA, CUBA

I couldn't believe the beauty of palm trees, blue waters, sunny skies, and the smiles of happy people as we landed at the port in Havana. What a paradise! Beauty all around. I fell in love with Cuba the first day I arrived. What does a 13-year-old know about her parents' life and ministry? All I knew was that I was on a new adventure!

We settled into the new alabaster home, built by funds donated by the Global Church of the Nazarene for the building of churches, parsonages, schools, and hospitals around the world. I was now in the seventh grade and my mother enrolled me in Calvert Course. I studied on my own with the help of tutors that corrected my work. They sent me tests which I returned by mail.

I learned much, even taking a course on Architecture. I always remember the "flying buttresses" of the buildings built during the Middle Ages. Not sure why that bit of information stuck, but it did!

I owned cats, dogs, pigeons, parakeets, and ducks. My favorite pet was a horse named, Manso [Tame]. When General Superintendent Williamson came to Cuba, he said, "This girl needs a horse."

That horse trusted me and never threw me off. He did everyone else that attempted to ride him. I enjoyed the long rides down the side road beside the Bible School grounds. I rode him a kilometer or two and then as I turned him around, I made him gallop all the way home. During the rainy season there were large potholes full of water. When we arrived home, we were both covered in mud from head to foot. But I loved the freedom of riding Manso to my heart's content through the beautiful Cuban countryside.

My brother Leon and I decided one day to dissect frogs [which multiplied at a more rapid pace than the infamous "frog plague" of the Moses' days in Egypt]. One of the frogs jumped away with his insides hanging out and his outer skin pulled back alongside his spinal cord. I felt sorry for him. That activity came to a sudden halt. I felt guilty for hurting the poor thing.

At 14, I began teaching a Sunday school class of girls. Before Sunday School, I walked the neighborhood, asking the parents if their children could accompany me to church. My class grew to 40 girls cramped in the upstairs classroom of the Mantilla Church. In 2016, I was able to return to

Cuba after 56 years, and my heart was thrilled to see that the church was alive and well.

My father oversaw the work in Cuba. A new church plant was organized, and a church building was built in La Ceiba, Marianao [adjacent city to Havana]. I played the piano and taught a Sunday School Class as well. I loved going to church and as a 16-year-old, I felt close to God, I loved Him and desired to serve Him. I never forgot my encounter with God at girls' camp.

My father took me on a piper cub plane to the Isle of Pines. Everyone there spoke English, even though it belonged to Cuba. He preached in the churches, and I played the piano. That was a fun trip with my dad.

"Besides riding your horse, what else did you do for fun during those years in Cuba? "I looked at this psychiatrist and wondered why he couldn't just let me finish the main points of my life story and get on with whatever was wrong with me.

I thought a bit and told him that we had teens at church that were my friends.

"What did you do for fun?"

Well, I thought some more, "I told you I rode my horse. I had pets."

"Did you go to any parties with your school friends?"

"No. that was a separate world. I went to school and came home. It was home, church, school, church, home."

"Well, go on. Tell me more."

I thought about an incredibly significant event in Cuba's timeline. But I didn't know if he would understand and I said, "There's something that happened but I don't think you will understand it."

"Well, try me." He smiled and repeated, "Go on."

BEAUTIFUL GUEST

If a man can be called 'beautiful' Eriberto was just that. As I played the piano one Sunday morning, a handsome young man wearing a suit walked into the back of the church and sat down. I was immediately struck by his good looks. Since he was a visitor, my parents invited him to our home for Sunday noon meal. That was the beginning of several visits he made to our home. Something new happened to my 16-year-old heart. I was infatuated with Eriberto. I now played the piano with the expectation of him coming in the church door. I began enjoying his visits to my home. I kept my heart news to myself, but secretly found I was now thinking of this handsome young man in my life. When no one was around he would wink at me and made me feel very special. But I told no one.

Why did you feel the need to keep it a secret?

I told him, "Because in Cuba, at that time, you didn't tell anyone you liked someone until it was official that you are actually boyfriend and girlfriend. And that was an entire process."

Thank you. Go ahead.

Playing the piano at church now was just perfunctory since all I wanted was to see my 24 -year-old heart throb. God seemed to move away, little by little. Something was not the same in my daily walk with God. This went on for several months and his visits and conversations with my father and Mother were long. They covered a long list of topics, from Christianity to Castro who was at the time was the new self-proclaimed Prime Minister in Cuba.

One day, while alone at home, I sensed I had to decide. My heart was torn and struggling. I locked my bedroom door and knelt at my bed. I told the Lord that he had to do something to help me because I knew that somehow Eriberto had replaced God as first in my life. So, I prayed long and hard and finally said, "I can't help it that you made women attracted to men and men to women. But I know that this man now has taken your place in my heart. So, until you take him out of my heart, I'll stay here and [drama Norma said] "Even if my flesh rots off my bones, I'll not get up until you take him out of my heart." And I meant it!

I don't know how long I stayed, but after some time, I felt at peace and got up and went on my way. Next Sunday, I found myself at the piano, praising God with my fingers and voice and when Eriberto walked in, I felt absolutely nothing for him. God had answered.

Tensions between Cuba and the United States was an understatement. The day arrived when my father received notice that the American Embassy was asking all US citizens to leave the island. There would be no more guarantees for American Citizens since diplomatic ties were being severed between both countries. That was a sad day! Three weeks later, we boarded a ship for Miami, leaving behind all personal belonging behind except 150 lbs. per person.

I cried most of the trip home. My mother asked me to come down and eat. I told her I just wanted to stay up on the bridge. I watched Havana's skyline fade slowing into the distance. I was sad and mad.

I loved Cuba and felt it was one place I felt was home. I relished the beauty of nature, the moonlit nights with the large, closer-to-the-Equator moons. I enjoyed writing poetry about the birds and animal life. The extroverted Cuban culture of that day was invigorating. My horse and I were friends and I missed him. All these components to my life in Cuba, made me feel that I truly "belonged". It was one of the saddest days in my young life. We left Cuba on August 12, my 17th birthday.

He listened intently. I didn't know what he thought. He jotted things down, then asked me to go on. I thought to myself, "These sessions are useless!" Telling my story wasn't doing a thing for either of us, so I thought!

CHAPTER VI

BETHANY, OKLAHOMA

*W*e settled on Redmond Street in the small town outside Oklahoma City. My brother Ray was now engaged to his fiancé, Claire Phillips and we were eager to meet her. Her father, Dr. E. S. Phillips was pastor of Bethany First Church of the Nazarene.

I enrolled in Bethany High School for my junior year. My adjustment to life in the United States was harsh and difficult. The teens my age seemed immature and silly. I dated a young man during my two years at Bethany. He had a car and I felt that he helped me adjust to living in the United States. Although I felt so out of place in my new environment, I thoroughly enjoyed two classes: typing [on electric typewriters!] and Drama. I could type fast because of my piano playing. And I could lose myself in acting and become someone I was not. These seemed to be my connectors to sensing I belonged somewhere in this new world. Except I was always given the role of a mother or an older woman! Esther was always the sexy, young thing! I was jealous!

One day my father received a letter from the leader of the church in Cuba. It read,

"We miss you so much but thank God you are safe. We found out that your name, Spurgeon, was on the list of counterrevolutionaries and you were going to be arrested. It's good you got out when you did. And guess who turned your name in? Yes, Eriberto! He was Castro's spy."

My heart sank then lifted in thanks to God! I was so glad I had obeyed!

On the day of my 18th birthday, my daddy surprised me by walking into the house with a dachshund puppy. He wore a sheepish grin as my mother looked at him with a chuckle and said, "Spurgeon!" I felt that my daddy knew some of the discomfort I was feeling, and he wanted to give me a gift. He knew I would really enjoy having a dog. As I was looking at the puppy in my dad's arms, he winked at me and so I named him, "Winkey".

My brother Leon was taking piano lessons. One day during his recital, I suddenly broke down crying. I didn't understand the reason for this outburst. I ran to the bathroom and shed tears and tears. My mother's questions brought no answer. "I don't know Mother! I don't know why I'm crying!"

Just before graduation, I broke up with my boyfriend, who told me he was going to "Mark Me" when I told him I didn't want to date him any longer. I thought to myself, "Buddy, just try it. You'll forever regret it is you so much as touch me!" I stared him down. He left me alone.

I went to my Senior prom with a new friend. He had been Oklahoma State Wrestling Champion. We dated for several months. He was exceedingly kind to me.

Following my High School Graduation, my mother told me that she heard about a job opening at the Bethany Police Department. She took me down for my interview. The Police and Fire Departments were just a block away from the college. My interview went well, and I'll never forget the ease with which Chief McClain affirmed me when he said, "Remember that that the only people who don't make mistakes are those residing at the cemetery. So, do your best and we'll be simply fine."

My duties were Court Clerk for Judge Showalter and part-time dispatcher for both fire and police departments. One of my highlights was being able to take my driving test in a Police Car. I passed it and was the proud owner of a Driver's License. Of course, No Car! But I lived in hopes of someday owning one.

BETHANY NAZARENE COLLEGE

I knew that my life was in transition. My parents were preparing to return to Argentina in August, and I was enrolled in summer classes at Bethany Nazarene College [Now Southern Nazarene University]. My boyfriend at that time helped me deal with the difficult days following their departure.

When I moved into the dorm, I remember thinking: "I've wallowed enough. I'm starting anew and will make the best of this situation". Classes and work kept me quite busy, and I was beginning to enjoy my newfound freedom.

However, there were days when I sought the help of Dr. Thurman Coburn, the School Psychologist. He was thoughtful and listened to my struggles with grief, loss, and depression. I never understood those moments when a cavern seemed to open and almost swallow me in fear and panic.

Most chapel times were filled with deep spiritual anointing. I loved listening to the preaching of Dr. E.S. Phillips, Pastor of Bethany First Church of the Nazarene. Those were years of spiritual growth as I heard some of the best preaching, I have ever heard. Yet outside the umbrella of the spiritual highs, I encountered a growing pattern of toxic fear and unmanageable anxiety.

My major was Education. I passed all the Spanish Courses and took several extra Bible Classes. During my sophomore year, Dr. E.S. and Gertrude Phillips allowed me to live with them while I studied and worked. I am grateful to them for their generosity in helping me during that year. I moved back into the dorm my junior year until our wedding day, November 24, 1964.

My brother Arlan Ray Hendrix had married Claire Christine Phillips and they lived in Bethany. This was a source of comfort to know my brother was close by.

I was working hard at taking ownership of my adjustment to college life in the United States. But deep inside, there existed that nomadic sense of moving, not staying long, not putting down stakes, for I soon would be moving on. I knew I was present in the moment, but I truly didn't belong.

CHAPTER VII

BONDING WITH BOB BRUNSON

*O*ne day in early November 1962, I was walking out of the dining hall at college when a young man approached me and said, "You are Norma Hendrix, aren't' you?" I said, "Yes". He continued, "I've heard a lot about you!" And then he proceeded to ask me out on a date on Sunday, November 4. We attended church and that marked the beginning of our courtship.

Bob was in his junior year, having transferred from Pasadena Nazarene College Pasadena, California, [Now Point Loma Nazarene University]. During his sopho-more year, he was reading the book, "Through Gates of Splendor", the story of the missionaries murdered by the Auca Indians in Ecuador. Bob recalled that he felt God asking him, "Would you be willing to be a missionary for me?" Bob related that he rolled off his bed, onto his knees and told the Lord, "Yes". He knew then that he was to serve the Lord in some foreign country.

Perhaps that was one of the drawing cards we had to each other, but I found the blond, blue-eyed young man enchanting and I fell in love with him. I don't think he knew how very culturally different I was from his American upbringing, but that didn't show up until later in marriage. He found out I was very Latin American in my way of thinking and socializing. On one date he said, "I can't wait to take you to eat tacos! I know you miss them."

I asked, "What is a taco?" In Spanish it means, "heel of shoe".

"You never ate a taco?"

"Nope, don't know what it is."

"Well, what did you eat in Argentina and Cuba?"

"Well not tacos! I ate raviolis, spaghetti, steaks, and potatoes. In Cuba, rice and beans and fried plantains."

I soon discovered what a "Taco" was.

I rode a bus out to California to visit his parents in Lynwood where his father was pastor. I fell in love with Freeman, Mildred and Bob's sister, Nancy immediately. They embraced me with the love of a future daughter-in-law, and I felt comfortable. Bob's brother, Ron was serving in Viet Nam at that time, and I met him later when he returned to the US.

Bob graduated with a Religion Major in May 1964. Immediately he began working on his master's at Bethany. In August of that year, Bob took the pastorate of a small rural church in Hydro, Oklahoma. After our wedding, I joined him, and we pastored that church for two years until

I graduated from college and then taught one year at John Glenn Elementary School in Oklahoma City.

BECOMING NORMA LOUISE HENDRIX-BRUNSON

We planned our wedding to take place at Bethany First Church of the Nazarene on Tuesday, November 24, 1964. We took the Thanksgiving break for our honeymoon. I'll never forget the sense I had of "this being God's will for me" as I walked down the aisle to marry Robert Worth Brunson. Dr. E.S. Phillips and Rev. Freeman Brunson officiated our wedding. My mother was able to come from Argentina, but my father and brother Leon could not. My brother Ray gave me away.

The night before our wedding, I had a crisis attack of fear. Bob and I tried to talk about it but all I could was cry. We returned to our apartment where my mother and I were staying. She was stunned at the tears and the discomfort between us. She asked what was wrong. We shared.

My mother surprised me. "Norma, I want you to go over to your fiancé, sit on his lap, put your arms around him, look him in the eye and tell him you love him and are glad to be his wife."

I was shocked. My mother, who had always told me to be careful, to not allow anything improper to come into my life, to be modest, sensible, and prudent was asking me to sit on my fiance's lap in her presence. Seemed out of character. But I complied. And all finished well.

He interrupted me. "It seems your mother held a great deal of control over you, doesn't it?" I looked at him and tried to respond respectfully. Inside I thought he was rude and impertinent, talking against my mother in that way!

"No," I replied, "I think she did exactly what I needed to have done."

"We'll come back to address that later."

"Like heck you will!" I thought to myself.

He read my body language. I continued.

We had over 600 people in attendance at our wedding. My friend Carolyn Macrory Riley lent me her beautiful wedding dress and Jan Yarbrough lent me her veil. We traveled to Hot Springs, Arkansas for our honeymoon and since it rained the entire time, we joked about not having anything to do during those days. We came back to Bethany and our apartment on Peniel Street and enjoyed opening out wedding gifts. People were so generous and kind to us.

BECOMING MRS. BRUNSON

I did my student teaching under the guidance of a lovely teacher-supervisor. She gave me high marks, but added, "One thing you need to do is be less harsh with the students." I felt I did an excellent job and I made them mind me. I guess I didn't see myself as she did. I thought about that comment many times.

My first teaching job was at John Glenn Elementary School in Oklahoma City. Barbara Baker and I were friends, and both taught 4th grade. The administration gave each teacher a wooden paddle which could be used in the extreme event of misconduct by a student. Only three swats were allowed, and another teacher had to be present.

One day, Barbara called me out to witness her much needed application of discipline upon a certain "Johnny". She stated firmly, "Johnny, bend over and grab your ankles."

"NO!" yelled Johnny.

"Johnny, I repeat, bend over and grab your ankles!"

"NO!" now Johnny is crying!

"Johnny, last time, bend over and grab your ankles and take this like a man!"

Johnny looks up with sobbing tears and says, "But I'm not a man!"

We both squelched our laughter as she pushed him down and gave him one swat. She sent him back into the room while we both erupted in laughter! Every time we met, even years later, we remembered that episode! "But I'm not a man!" Right, he was, and we truthfully behaved shamelessly! We should have been swatted!

BECOMING A PASTOR'S WIFE

On Wednesday nights and on weekends we traveled the 60 miles to our new pastorate, Church of the Nazarene in Hydro, Oklahoma. The people were so patient and gentle with us. There was a parsonage where we stayed over the weekends. Jackie and Merrietta Miller were the key helpers as we learned the ropes. Several years later, Bob was called back to hold a funeral for one of the members that had been so close a friend during those two years at Hydro. There were several churches in town, so we did quite well with the 40 or 50 in attendance.

The people were kind-hearted. But I was uncomfortable. I felt out of control. I didn't understand this rural environment. My city-life experience contrasted with the slow, rural, farm life of the United States. I learned that life moved more slowly, and people spent more time with each other. The town cafe entertained the town folk that just wanted to come and "shoot the breeze". I felt that it was "wasting time", since we "need to get things done". That still percolates within me. I need to remember some of the great lessons I learned as a new member of the Hydro community.

And I was adjusting to the man I married. And he to me. He needed to be in control, and so did I. I played the piano, he preached. He organized meetings, parties, and services. I felt I could do as good a job. The struggle began. We didn't understand the dynamics that were building, but they were there.

Another interruption. "Tell me about your husband's parents".

"Well, his father was very dominant. He was kind and helpful, but he oversaw everything in the home. His mother

did whatever her husband wanted. She was more compliant. She's an awesome cook. Her house is immaculate, and everything is in its place and every place has its thing." And I added, "They were pastors in California. He has passed away.

CHAPTER VIII

BACK TO MOVING

*I*n 1967, we moved to Kansas City. Missouri, so Bob could attend Nazarene Theological Seminary. We packed up our belongings and relocated to a little house right across from a cemetery. We lived close to the Seminary.

Our relationship was becoming more comfortable as we learned to talk things out. But in a sense, now we lived in two worlds: he at seminary and I at school.

I began teaching at Stony Point Elementary School in Kansas City, Kansas. My school principal was a wonderful godly man who gave me support and helped me learn the ropes of teaching in a new school district. Bob and I learned a lot about understanding each other.

My first year was the toughest since I had 36 third graders, full of energy and who were street-smart. My supervisor at the time was Miss Titt and when I had to introduce her, I tried to skillfully slide over her name so the kids would not laugh. She decided to write her name on the board. As soon as she did, they burst out laughing!

She didn't take to me or the class very well, and I must say that some of the teachers in the lounge that day laughed and said, "The best she could do would be change her name to Bosom!"

I learned to drink coffee at Stony Point. My other choice was smoking. The teachers' lounge was always full of smoking and coffee drinking. Sometimes it was hard to see the coffee pot because the smoke was so thick.

BEWILDERED

For a couple of months, my monthly visitor did not appear. Bob was in his second year at Seminary and the only reason he could attend was that I carried the weight of the income. He was working part time first at a grocery store and then at General Motors. But health insurance and rent were on my shoulders. I was also concerned because at that time pregnant women had to quit working as soon as they began showing. I was afraid and did not know how this would work out. Anxiety was building.

One day while reading to the 4th and 5th grade students, I started feeling excruciating menstrual pain. I asked a fellow teacher to please take the children to their lunch time. I made it to the principal's office.

The nurse was in her cubicle. I ran past her into the restroom. I was in so much pain that I barely made it to the toilet. I saw the flow of blood, gushing out into the bowl. I grimaced in the extreme pain and knew then, that a large clot had dislodged itself as it fell into the stool. I continued bleeding profusely. I stuffed myself full of toilet paper to attempt at stopping the bleeding. After flushing the stool, I walked into the principal's office and told him I was sick and needed to go home.

We lived 20 miles away. I felt weak as I drove, and continued bleeding. It was about 1:00 p.m. when I arrived home. Bob was at the Seminary. I ran into my bathroom. I left a trail of blood from the car to the bathroom. My thought was, "I'll wait until Bob gets home". But as the bleeding continued, I felt it necessary to call my sister-in-law, Claire Hendrix. She came and immediately got in touch with Bob. [No cell phones then]. He came quickly and took me to the doctor. He confirmed that I had miscarried. I took a week off and returned to work relieved that I had not messed up our plans for seminary and then the mission field.

I admit that to this day I am baffled with my gut reaction to the entire miscarriage crisis. I did not mourn or grieve. I was relieved that I was not pregnant. I was eager to get back to life as normal; Norma teaching school and Bob studying at seminary. I did not want the complication of a child at that time. Several women offered me grief support and comfort which somehow missed the mark with my true feelings about the matter.

He stopped me again. "Do you want to talk more about your feelings during that time?"

I tried to explain that we had a goal in mind and did not want to be deterred: Bob to finish Seminary and then go to the "Mission Field". He asked, "What do you mean 'Mission Field'?" I explained.

"Continue."

Bob and I were assigned as Youth Pastors and Bob as music director at Grace Church of the Nazarene in Independence, Missouri. That was a good time of preparation while Bob studied, and I worked.

In May of 1967, Bob was Ordained as Elder in the Church of the Nazarene. His father was able to hand his son the certificate of Ordination and Dr. E. H. Lewis ordained him. That was a red-letter day in our lives.

BOARD MEETING WITH THE DEPARTMENT OF WORLD MISSION – CHURCH OF THE NAZARENE

Bob and I applied as missionaries to the Department of World Mission. Subsequently we were appointed by the Board of General Superintendents to Peru. Our sending service at College Church of the Nazarene in Kankakee, Illinois was a highlight I'll never forget. There were 40 of us, the largest sending group ever sent by the Church of the Nazarene. When the song, "So Send I You" was sung, the tears flowed and the commitments stood clear and strong: "Lord, we will go where you want us to go and do what you want us to do." We meant it. It was easy to say. Life would show it's quite another commitment to continue saying it and mean it.

We packed our earthly belongings into nine large, metal barrels. Now when Bob did something, he did it to perfection. One of his perfectionistic accomplishments was to solder the top rings shut. A year later, when we received our shipment in Peru, customs agents tried to open the rings and they worked and worked but they could not. So, Bob had the most rewarding job of prying open nine barrels containing our earthly goods! I think he was sorry he did such a perfect job!

CHAPTER IX

BOUND FOR MEXICO CITY AND LANGUAGE STUDY

*W*e were first assigned to Mexico City for a Bob's language study. We left from Los Angeles International Airport in August of 1970. It was difficult saying good-bye to Bob's parents. They both cried as we hugged good-bye. Bob's father said, "I am so proud of you son, answering God's call on your life."

My parents were in Argentina. As I remember, we communicated once a month by letter. They loved us, but we were in two different worlds. I didn't know much about their lives and they didn't know much about ours.

We landed in Mexico City to the noise, confusion, and traffic of that huge city. And suddenly I felt I belonged. I knew the language, some of the customs, the noise and yes, the bars on doors and windows were simply part of the architecture.

As we arrived at our apartment, we walked through a metal gate which was attached to the metal bars surrounding our apartment. When the gate clanged shut, Bob remarked, "Man, I feel like I'm in jail!" I was startled by that remark because I answered, "That's strange! I feel safe for the first time since I left Cuba!" The open yards in the United States always made me feel exposed and in danger.

I was afraid he would stop me after that last comment, like, "You are telling me you felt afraid in open yards in the States?" but he didn't.

Bob enrolled in the Language School located in the "Zona Rosa" [Pink Zone]. I had the opportunity to play for a quartet called "Los Nazarenos", who traveled around singing in different churches. They were able to cut their second record. I was their pianist.

Bob and I rode the bus for two hours across Mexico City to attend Sunday church. Of course, we arrived on time, at 9:00 am. But people started flocking in at 9:45 am. Sunday School and Church dragged on until 1:00. I was bored to death, and I felt for Bob who was just beginning to learn the language. It harked back to my church years in Argentina! Why did church have to be so long! So boring!

I played the piano. It's a wonder I'm not deaf! A little man played the violin and stood over my right shoulder, shrieking, and screeching his violin strings in my ear! I was invited to play the piano at a church rally. I was relieved because I knew the "violin man wouldn't be there!" And sure enough, as soon as I started playing, here he came, violin and all!

Bus rides were infamous. Crowded with people standing body to body made getting a seat the joy of the day! Bob's youth and American appeal drew women's attention. One day, while he was not wearing his wedding band, [at that time, ministers in our denomination did not wear wedding bands] a woman forcefully pushed herself against him asking if she could get to know him better. He stated, "I'm Married!" She started laughing, "Oh, and bad boy! Not wearing your wedding band!" I quickly told Bob, "Hey buster, we's getting a wedding band today!" He laughed and said, "Yep, that's a good idea!" He wore it till the end.

Bob finalized his studies and graduated with good grades. We set a four-hour time frame every day when we only spoke Spanish. I felt in control once again. My culture. My language. I had an "up" on the situation. During my year in Mexico City, I never once felt that gaping hole of depression and fear.

BOUND FOR LIMA PERU

In August of 1971 we boarded a Braniff flight to Lima, Peru. We left the warmth of Mexico City to arrive on a cold, dreary, cloud covered, misty morning in Lima. The shocking contrast hit me like a brick wall. The cold, damp air curled up my hair and froze my bones. Missionaries

Clyde Golliher and Howard Grantz greeted us at the airport and drove us to our apartment. Although the weather was unwelcoming, our missionary friends made us feel right at home. We were excited to finally be at our post.

BUILDING FROM SCRATCH

Our assignment involved church planting in a new area of Lima called San Martin de Porras. Most of the people in that large area had come to Lima from the mountain areas to get better jobs. But their living conditions as squatters was horrendous. Little by little the people had begun to build their homes, one brick at a time. I admired their resilience.

The city provided large barrels [like the ones Bob soldered!] and placed one by a group of huts. Once a week a water truck drove through to fill each barrel. Home, for most, consisted of four reed mats, held up by stakes. There was little need for a roof since it seldom rains in Lima. A light misty, sort of humidity, blankets the atmosphere with moisture called "garua".

Our first task was to find a proper location for a new church plant. We were able to secure a corner building that had once been a bar. Large metal doors rolled up and down for security. We organized the church with a handful of believers that had found the Lord through our First Church of the Nazarene in Lima, but who lived close to our new location.

The first Sunday was exciting with 16 people in attendance. We announced with large posters and flyers that we were starting a new church plant and the showing of a Christian Film. That was a thrilling time with people lined up outside and inside watching the film. Little by little people began coming to faith in Jesus Christ. Lives were changed and we were able to see the church organized as The San Martin de Porras Iglesia del Nazareno.

Interruption time: "How was your husband adjusting to another set of cultural realities? And how was your relationship?"

I thought, then spoke, "I think he was becoming reliant on me to help him understand if he didn't quite get the meaning of someone's comment. Or he didn't understand the cultural cues. Sometimes, I sensed he was really stressed and especially with the driving. He expected people to drive better. He was angry much of the time while driving. I told him once, 'I'd rather let them be wrong, than us dead, Bob!'"

I also added, that truthfully, the Peruvian culture was quite different from either culture in which I had lived, so I was learning as well.

BEAUTIFUL PEOPLE OF GOD

One of the new Christians was a lady whose husband had left her to care for the child of his mistress. She raised that little girl and at the time the little girl, Maria, was 7 years old. Maria walked in one Sunday, with Mrs. Palomino who held a baby. She shared that her ex-husband had brought her another baby to raise, from another mistress. She was poor and needy. The church helped her, and she came to faith in Jesus Christ. As she grew in her faith, I came to know her well. She shared that she had been a famous dancer and showed me albums full of her youth and dance outfits. But she said, "I grew old and then I lost all my income."

One day she asked me to visit her. Upon arrival she stated,

"I want to come to church on Sunday and leave something on the altar. I want to give this to God."

She opened a trunk and showed me several statues: Mary, Baby Jesus, San Martin de Porras and others. Mrs. Palomino continued, "Now that I have accepted Jesus, I don't need these anymore and I want to put them on the altar."

Next Sunday she came to church. Maria held the baby. Mrs. Palomino had a large bag. When altar time came, she got up and one by one laid them on the altar and told me, "You take care of them. I don't need them anymore."

I was constantly baffled by the poverty around me in this area of Peru. I felt so useless. Impetigo, lice, worms, open sores, runny noses, and other health issues overwhelmed me. Our resources were so limited.

One day, as we drove to church, my heart was heavy, and I desired nothing more than to run away from all the chaos, poverty, and the sense of my inability to change the situation around me. I privately told the Lord, "Father, I can't do this anymore. I am making no difference by being here. I can't help these people. They are poor. They are hungry. They are sick. I can do absolutely nothing to change their status quo. Why am I even here?"

Just as we drove over the railroad tracks, I sensed the Lord say to me, "Norma, I didn't send you here to change things. I sent you here to love them and show them I love them."

From that day forward, I began to love them with all the love I had for the Lord. I did what I could to help them, bringing help as we could while showing them the way to real life in Christ. Although my feeling of belonging was growing, I knew I had a long way to go before I could truly get into the hearts of my fellow Peruvians.

My session was over, and I returned to my room. The routine continued.

CHAPTER X

BLESSED IN PRAYER

*O*ne day in early April 1973, I was upstairs in my room praying. I had just returned from taking a new Christian girl on a 500-mile bus ride up to the Seminary in Chiclayo. I was thankful that Ella had decided to follow Jesus. So, in prayer, I felt only praise and joy in the Lord. As I was in prayer, suddenly out of nowhere I had this extraordinarily strong impression, "Norma, a year from this Mother's Day [May] You will be a mother."

Bob and I had been married nine years by now, and I had only had the one pregnancy which ended in miscarriage. I ran downstairs and calmly said, "Bob, a year from this mothers' day, I will be a mother." His first response was, "Now, Norma, please don't get your hopes up. You know you're always dis-appointed!" My retort, "I know what I know."

BRUNSON BABY GIRL – MIRACLE #1

I made an appointment with my gynecologist at the Anglo-American Clinic. When he saw me, he was curious as to why I had made the appointment. I said, "I'm pregnant." He looked at me with unbelief and said, "I really doubt that you are, but if you are, please know you will not be able to carry this child." I had been diagnosed with a bicornate uterus, too thin and too small to carry a baby full term. I looked at him and said, "Please give me a pregnancy test." Which he did.

Two days later he called me to tell me that indeed, I was pregnant. But repeated warnings that for sure there was no way I would have this child. I said, "I believe in God's power to give me this child."

Two weeks later I began bleeding profusely. The doctor hospitalized me for a week and sent me home to complete bed rest until the bleeding stopped. For the first seven months, I was confined to the bedroom where God had given me the assurance that I was going to be a mother. I spent the time knitting, reading, watching TV on a little black and white television. I learned all about Peruvian music, Andean flute sounds, and the news. Not much else on television those days.

Once a month, Bob carried me down the stairs for the ride to my doctor's appointment. I'll never forget the joy I had at being outside, seeing and hearing the sights and sounds of the bustling city. The flowers on the vending carts brought life to my soul.

Bob had much responsibility during that time. He was caring for two congregations, San Martin de Porras and the Collique church. He was gone most of the day but would come home fix lunch and then leave again. Those were interesting months, as I waited with expectant joy at the birth of my child. I somehow knew what Mary felt "as she pondered those things in her heart." I wasn't going to birth the Messiah, but I sure was going to give birth to God's miracle in my life! And that set me to much pondering!

Robin Michelle Brunson was born by C-section on December 18, 1973, and yes, I celebrated the next Mothers' Day in full form. She was my first and last full-term pregnancy. I belonged to that little girl, and she sure belonged to me. Bob couldn't hold and contain his joy at finally having a daughter which we had so longed for.

When Robin was about nine months old, Dr. Larry Garman, invited Bob and me to the jungle to teach in the Bible Training School. We left our car in Chiclayo and rode a bus for 18 hours up over the Andes mountains down on the eastern slope and then into the jungle areas. The ride was rough and bumpy. Teofila and I took turns holding Robin. Bob had the unprecedented honor of sitting on a small stool in the aisle while holding on the nearest secure pole.

We stayed overnight in a small town of Bagua Chica and arrived in time to attend the service at the little Nazarene church in town. I remember thinking, "It would take months for anyone to find out what happened to us if we had an accident or suffered some tragedy. We are at the end of the world here!"

That night, I noticed an American lady in church. After the service I went to introduce myself and asked her where she was from. She said, "Well, I was born in Ringwood, Oklahoma but I've lived elsewhere during my life. I'm heading back into the jungle to visit some Swiss Missionaries." I couldn't believe that there, in the middle of the Peruvian Jungle, I would meet a woman born in the little Oklahoma town, birthplace of my mother!

The small boat carried us down river to the mission station. Bob taught classes and was involved in baptizing several new believers in the Marañon River. I helped Larry arrange and clean out some of the areas in his small clinic area.

Our time was up. As we were loading the boat to head upriver, Larry asked if we could take several wooden boxes back to Lima with us. His grin caught us off guard. Bob said we would and then asked, "What's in the boxes?"

Larry explained that the Peruvian government pays the Aguarunas 10 USD each for capturing the most dangerous snake in the jungle, the Shushupe. [Bushmaster Snake]. According to Britannica, it is the "longest venomous snake in the New World". Once captured, they are placed in small wooden crates and taken to a laboratory in Lima. Their poison is milked, then injected into horses, donkeys, or other mammals to create an antivenom.

Bob agreed. We climbed into the small canoe to make our way up the Marañon River to Bagua Chica. We boarded the bus for the long ride back to Chiclayo. At this time, the Peruvian government had imposed a nationwide ration on gasoline. Every car had a red or white windshield sticker.

We could only drive on Wednesdays, Fridays, and Sundays. We arrived in Chiclayo early Wednesday morning. Curfew started at 2:00 am of the day you could drive and ended at 2:00 am of the next day.

BOXES WITH WHAT?

We loaded our belongings into our Chevy carryall, including the boxes holding 12 Shushupe snakes, and headed down the two-lane Pan-American Highway towards Lima. Bob soon noticed that the generator light was on. He drove to a garage. By the time the car was repaired, it was 1:00 pm. We debated whether to stay in Chiclayo overnight and then back to Lima on Friday. We were exhausted and needed rest. But Bob said, "We need to get to Lima because we have prayer meeting." So, we left Chiclayo for the eight-to-ten-hour drive back to Lima. The night was cold, so we put the car heater on high.

I was buckled up and had fallen asleep with my head on Bob's lap. Robin was secured in her bed in the back seat. I awoke with a start as we were spinning off the road. Robin was screaming. The front of our car was totally crushed. Bob was slumped over the steering wheel. Steam was spewing from the motor. I tried to open my passenger's door, but it was smashed in. My arm didn't work. I tried to push myself over the seat to reach my wailing daughter while I yelled, "Bob! Bob!" He seemed to awaken. He got out of his side and walked around moaning. Suddenly in the darkness I saw a man walk up to the car. I yelled at him in Spanish, "Señor, Señor, I don't know who you are but please have mercy and get my little girl in the back seat!" By that time Bob was aware and he came to the car, picked her up and held her tightly.

I couldn't move. Bob and the truck driver were trying to see how they could pry my door open, but it was too accordioned and crushed. I finally laid down under the bent steering wheel and asked them to pull me out by my left arm. The pain was intense as they tried to keep my body straight. Something was broken but didn't know what. They laid me down on the sand by the car. I was shivering with the cold, desert wind.

I looked up at the black sky. No moon. No stars. And I sensed, no God. This was the first time in my life that I felt God had abandoned us. My feelings were real. My body hurting, the cold gritty sand across my back and arms, and the cries of my little girl all bore down on me with despair. I felt myself slipping into a large hole.

Bob was coming out of his daze and saw that we had hit the back of a truck carrying ten tons of oranges. Bob had tried to pass but had dozed off just as he was passing. The passengers' side of the car was totally crushed in. Later we realized had I been sitting up it would have probably killed me. Bob sustained broken ribs and a forehead cut. I suffered five pelvic fractures, a broken arm, and a shattered hip socket. The side door bar had cut a huge gash in my right hip. Robin did not have a scratch on her although her bed was full of broken glass.

The truck driver tried to wave down an occasional car. No one would stop. Finally, he came to me and said, "Señora, I've stopped a car and they will take you to the nearest clinic. Don't moan or groan or they will throw you out onto the highway. They don't want to be accused of causing the wreck." He and Bob picked me up and scrunched me into the back seat with Bob and Robin. I was in pain! Just as Bob climbed in the man said, "I'll watch your belongings until someone comes to get your things." And Bob, in all the confusion, had the wisdom to say, "And oh yes, be careful. We are carrying 12 Shushupe snakes to Lima. I don't know if they got out or not!"

The man's eyes widened! Shushupes?! And when at daybreak missionaries arrived at the site to pick up our belongings, the truck driver was sitting on top of the truck, watching our car! Our car was totaled. We recovered our belongings, and the snakes did make it to the laboratory!

We were hospitalized in Lima, Bob for a few days until he felt he could breathe with less pain. The X rays showed that I could not walk because the hip socket was, "Shattered like a hard-boiled eggshell. No walking for three months! And arm in a cast from below wrist to above elbow."

Bob and I were crushed. We felt defeated and ashamed that we had caused such problems for the mission, for the church and for our own lives. We were both hospitalized in the same room. I was in one of those dark times. I missed my baby. I tried not to blame Bob.

One day, a long-time friend, Ron Denton, who happened to be in Lima for a meeting of the Bible Society, walked in. If you knew Ron, you knew he was loud, mischievous, a jokester and loved to pull pranks on people. But not this day. He walked in with a sense of peace and love. He told us the story.

"There was a family who lived between two mountains. They had one son. One day the father realized that his son had never seen a sunrise. So, he decided to take his son up to the summit. They packed their tent and belongings and trekked up the steep slopes and arrived in the late afternoon. Tent set up; they fell asleep. Early the next morning, the father was awakened by the son yelling, "Dad, Dad! Come here, the world is coming to an end! Look the world is on fire!" The father went out and gently answered, "No son, the world is not coming to an end. It's the beginning of a new day."

We both wept. I can't remember a moment when God's timing in our lives was more evident as that visit from an old friend we hadn't seen in years.

For one month and a half, I lay in bed. Then I could sit in the wheelchair. Bob carried me down the stairs and placed me in the chair during the day. At night he took me back upstairs. The most uncomfortable part of it all was the itching inside my arm cast! I finally took a knitting needle, cut a hole in the elbow part of the cast, and used the needle to scratch where it itched!

The worst part of it all was that I couldn't really take care of my little girl. I thanked God that my mother was able to care for us until I was able to get into the wheelchair. She and my father were serving as missionaries in Uruguay at that time. My mother and Bob were great, but I longed for the time when I could begin caring for my beautiful, blond baby girl.

CHAPTER XI

BOUND FOR HOME ASSIGNMENT

*H*ealing took place and we were able to resume our duties. Our first term ended, and we left for the States to begin our year-long home assignment. For one trimester that year, Bob taught at Trevecca Nazarene University in Nashville, Tennessee. We lived on campus and enjoyed being close to Bob's sister and husband, Dr. Hal, and Nancy Cauthron. I appreciated the time to read and rest. One of Catherine Marshal's book deeply spoke to my heart.

BECKONING DREAM

One day, after reading, I fell asleep and dreamed. I found myself in a dingy room, full of boxes and stuff. The windows were dirty, and the shades were pulled half-way down. There was one naked lightbulb hanging from the ceiling. In the middle of that dark room junky room was a large steamer trunk. And sitting on top of that trunk was Norma. She was dressed in loud clothes and flaunted herself with jewelry and Self. Suddenly Norma seemed to say, "Wow, look at this room! Full of all this junk! Man, I hate all this stuff! Jesus, can you help me get rid of all this stuff?"

It seemed I heard his voice from outside the room. "Norma, I want to clean your room, but you need to come out and let me in." So, I said, "Sure, come on in. I'll wait outside." Some time went by while I waited in a hallway. Suddenly the door opened, and Jesus said, "Come on in". I walked into a large, round room, with clean, sparkling windows all around. The walls were a bright yellow and the floor was beautifully polished wood. There were no boxes or trunks insight. And I heard Jesus say, "You see this room, Norma? It's clean. It sparkles. The windows are clear. And I am here with you. If you want me to stay, then this room is only for you and me. Nothing else can come in. If it does, I leave. This is your heart, and all the stuff is gone. I love you."

I awoke in tears. I knew what some of the "stuff" was. I had been hurt by comments. We had been truncated at times from carrying out some of the ideas we had for ministry. There was criticism and gossip. And I was resentful. I resented many people, including my husband. I bowed my knees and confessed that I wanted all the stuff out of my heart. I wrote a long letter to people that I felt had hurt me. I forgave them. I told them I was sorry for my attitude. The letter was long. The tears fell. My heart was open, and the Holy Spirit was doing a work in me. I cried tears of shame, of repentance and took in all that God had for me at that moment. And I felt clean, new, and alive. I praised him until I could praise him no longer. Then I took the letter, read it again out loud and tore it up in many pieces. I was free. When Bob came home for dinner, he found his wife with a transformed heart. I shared my heart with him. We had a great time of bonding and understanding.

BUT LORD REALLY?

Our first home assignment year was nearing an end. Our travels took us all over the United States speaking in Missionary Conventions, Faith Promise Conventions, Zone Rallies, Chapels and Youth Conferences.

God helped me set up a skit that we used many times. I dressed in the Peruvian garb of a woman of the Andes who had come to Christ. It became an effective communication tool to show people some of the daily dress, customs and at the same time tell the story of Christ's redeeming grace.

Our first term had been fulfilling, but difficult. But the accident and some of the negative memories hung tightly around my psyche. Secretly, I wanted to be transferred to another field. I prayed quietly all that year, asking God to change our assignment or change me. One month out, we were headed to Peru. Two weeks out, we were headed to

Peru. One hour out of Lima on our return trip, we were about to land in Peru!

Our second term in Peru was the best we could have imagined. Bob oversaw starting the extension Seminary in Lima, plus traveling to the Andean areas to teach classes. Many times, he stood for hours in the back of a large truck, surrounded by men going to their work locations. The roads were narrow as they made their way out across the rugged Andes Mountains. The cold penetrated one's very bones. Bob's riding companions found that chewing coca leaves helped ward off the cold! I'm glad Bob never took up the practice. I sure wasn't going to kiss him with green teeth!

It was January 1978. One day I asked the Lord, if it were possible, for Bob and me to adopt a baby. I had gone through so much with the pregnancy, and I knew there were many children that were adoptable. I started asking God for an adoption, rather than a pregnancy.

At first, Bob was against the idea. His father's health was deteriorating, and Bob didn't know when he would need to go see his father in California. Bob also felt the process would take much time, energy, and finances. And he was fully invested in starting up the Extension Bible Training Program in Lima.

My prayer, as well as my conversations regarding the matter, continued month after month. In August, I spoke to Bob again and he adamantly said, "Norma, I have told you and will tell you for the last time, this is not what I have the energy to think about and plan for right now, Please, don't talk to me about it again."

I went to prayer. I was contrite before the Lord, "I can't help it that you have given me these maternal instincts. I can't help it that I really do not want to raise a child by herself. I would like for Robin to have a sibling, preferably a baby girl. So, Lord, this is the last time I'm praying about this. Either change Bob or change me. Thank you for listening. Amen." I forgot about the issue and continued busy with my missionary assignments and home activities.

During that time, I played the piano for the singing group, Acompañame. We laughed together, practiced together, prayed together, and traveled to different churches presenting the message in song. We were able to cut a tape in a recording studio. Many people in the churches loved to listen to their voices blend in praise.

One of the highlights for us was our invitation to sing on National Peruvian TV. We were scheduled on the day that the pope died. When we arrived at the radio station, the manager told us that it would not be advisable for them to sing, since the nation was in mourning. I popped up and said, "But they are singing, 'He died for me'. He responded, "Oh well, then yes, they can go ahead and sing." Which they did. I had translated the lyrics of the hymn, written by Mosie Lister, "His Grace is Sufficient", but in Spanish I used the title, "He Died for Me". We all chuckled later when we realized that the title permitted them to sing on television. Otherwise, they would have been turned away. God was chuckling too, I think!

BIRDS AND BOAS

I was director of the Bible School Choir in Chiclayo. One day, as we were practicing "His Eye is on the Sparrow, [in Spanish it is translated, "If he cares for the birds, He will also care for you."] I thought about my pet pigeon. I asked them if they were amenable to using the pigeon in the song. They were all on board. So, the practice was that before we sang the hymn, someone took the bird out of the cage, wrapped a ribbon around its foot and tied it to the girl's hand she held behind her back.

We practiced and practiced. The pigeon was picture perfect! As the choir bellowed out, "If He Cares for the Birds!"... her arm raised up high with the pigeon beautifully poised on top of her hand. The oohs and aahhs in the crowds were heartwarming. Except one time.

We were singing in Tucuman, Peru. The town theatre was at our disposal. We sang to a full house. Time for the pigeon to appear. "He Cares for the Birds!", and Rosa lists her arm high, and the bird feels the need for bathroom release!

The choir starts giggling and so do the people sitting close to the stage. I'm pumping away at the pump organ pedals while saying, "Just keep singing! Just keep singing!"

74

Rosa didn't know what to do with the gunk streaming down her arm.

After the concert, we had a talk. "Do you want the pigeon or not?" "Yes! Yes!" they all said. I told them then, that if it occurred again, they had to keep singing as if nothing happened. And it did and they did not. Next time, the girl next to Rosa, had a Kleenex handy and just wiped Rosa's arm while she sang away. That pigeon knew when to mess up!

I also had a pet boa constrictor. Don't know why, but then the "pet" issue is probably why. Animals are interesting to me. One day I needed to present a Sunday School lesson at the Monsefu Nazarene Church. I came up with the incredibly creative idea to use the snake. I had part of the lesson in my head.

Then I thought of my pigeon. "Great! Snake – Devil; Pigeon – Holy Spirit of God.

Two boxes. One wrapped beautifully and the other plainly. Snake in a colorful box. Holy Spirit in plain, white box. And the analogy would be something like,

"The enemy of our soul paints sin beautifully. But when you open the box, you find out that you get bit and poisoned. The Holy Spirit of God comes to us patiently, softly, and gently and tells us to avoid the dangers. He invites us to a life of joy and peace."

I had my boxes all ready. On Saturday, something told me, "I think I should practice this". So, I went to the snake cage and stuck my hand in, which I had done many times to feed it. But today, as I reached in, it bit me. I slung that snake clear across the room. It hit the wall and slid down to the floor and just stayed there. I later learned that when shedding, they are partially blind. They strike out of fear during shedding time at any object that threatens them.

Now the snake is on the floor, and I need to get it back in its cage. Broom helped. Snake back in cage. But fingers are swelling. I headed over to the ER and got a shot, and fingers sterilized. Yeah, that lesson never came to fruition. Had it, not only would the snake be out of the cage, but the entire congregation would also have run out of the church. I was unaware of how terribly frightened Peruvians were of all snakes. Boas are not poisonous. They just constrict and can kill a human if they get large. Mine was about three feet in length.

BABY PUPPIES

One day we came home at about 7:00 pm. A box was lying at our front door. No, it wasn't FEDEX. I opened it and found four newborn female puppies with umbilical cords still attached. I felt sorry for them. They were yelping and hungry.

I took them inside and began feeding them with warm milk and an eye dropper. Well, that took some time! 11:00 p.m. and I was still feeding them. I thought of our dachshund Snoopy, in the back yard. She had given birth to puppies three years before and had been in our backyard all the time. "Perhaps, Snoopy will take care of them." I brought her in and put a puppy close to her. Snoopy started growling and snarling. She walked away and growled at me!

Well, I knew I was not going to be able to care for four puppies. At midnight, I took the puppies into the washroom where Snoopy slept and laid them in their box. Snoopy was snarling. Puppies were squirming and squealing.

As I laid my head on my pillow, I said a quick prayer, "Lord, you love your creation. Could you somehow fill their little stomachs with milk? I don't have time to be feeding puppies!" And I fell asleep.

At 3:00 am I am awakened by screaming puppies. I went to the kitchen, heated some milk, and headed to the washroom. Snoopy was in her bed asleep, and the puppies in their bed yelping. I picked up the first one. Suddenly, I decided to try getting Snoopy to help me. I brought a puppy close to her and she growled. I pushed her head down and brought the puppy closer. She snarled. Something told me to put milk on her one of her teats. Which I did. While holding Snoopy's head with my left hand, I put the puppy up to her teat and it grabbed on and started sucking. Growl! Growl! Drink! Drink! [Puppy wouldn't let go] So I did the same with the other three.

Snoopy slowly quit grumbling and started sniffing. Little by little I let go of her head. She reached over and started smelling the puppies. No more growling. She started licking and cleaning them. She suddenly took ownership of these stray puppies. In three days, her bags were dragging

the floor and she literally raised them. They became known
as the "miracle puppies".

CHAPTER XII

BRUNSON BABY GIRL – MIRACLE #2

One November morning in 1978, we received a call from our friend, Mary Li, RN at the Anglo-American Clinic. She conveyed an interesting phone message. After hanging up, I calmly went to Bob who had just arrived home for lunch.

"Bob, Mary Li called and says that a first has happened at the Clinic. A wealthy woman came, gave birth to a baby girl five days ago and left. Before leaving, she said that a family member would pick up the child. But no one has come, and the clinic wants someone to adopt the baby. Mary Li wanted me to ask us if we would consider it."

Bob looked at me silently. He slowly answered me, "Let's have lunch, then we'll go pray about it." Lunch time that day was quiet. I already knew the answer. I was just waiting for Bob to find it out too. We took Robin into his office, knelt and Bob began to pray a beautiful prayer, asking God for direction and leadership in this issue. We spent quite a long time, silently pondering, praying, listening. Finally, Bob said, "Okay, let's go see her."

Rather than feeling exuberance and joy, I sensed, peace and calm. I was unusually quiet and pensive, wondering how we would convey this information to the Department of World Mission. We also knew that the expenses would be on our shoulders, for unlike a biological birth, we would be responsible for any expenses incurred in medical and adoption bills.

Our first sight of the beautiful baby was thrilling. Bob's first words were, "Isn't she beautiful?" I took her in my arms and prayed over her. I asked God to make it clear as to whether we should adopt her. I asked God to pave the way for World Mission to give us the green light. I unwrapped her blankets and looked at her little body, all beautifully made. I was filled with joy.

Bob and I went to another room and discussed it. Bob said, "I believe this is God's will for us. But I need to call headquarters and ask permission." We told the hospital authorities that we would be back tomorrow to take her home and begin the adoption process. When we arrived home. Bob made several phone calls to Kansas City. Secretary Esther McNutt answered the phone and told us that all the General Superintendents were out of the country, and she was not able to reach any of them by phone. [The days before the internet, texting, e-mails!]. But Esther added, "I have adopted children, so I am going to tell you, 'Go ahead and bring her home and adopt her!'"

November the 4th was a beautiful day. We always remembered that it marked our first date and now, the day that we brought Sheri home to be our own daughter. What a day that was! We began the process through first finding a lawyer. The first one gave us several options to facilitate the adoption. First option: "Senora, you can say that you had an affair with a Peruvian and this is the result of your pregnancy." Second option, "You can say that the baby was left on your doorstep."

Bob and I looked at each other and smiled. I said, "No, we are starting with the truth and the truth will prevail. She was born at the Anglo-American Clinic and the mother wishes for the child to be adopted, since she has signed her rights away."

A friend told us that a judge in Callao, would help us and only charge $75 USD. And he did. In one month to the day, our daughter whom we named, Sheri Renae Brunson, was legally adopted by Peruvian law. God always had a perfect plan. God had answered my prayer! I was ecstatic!

BOUND FOR HOME ASSIGNMENT -1979

Bob was enrolled at Fuller Seminary in Pasadena, California, to work on a Masters in Old Testament. So, we scheduled a place to live at Casa Robles Retirement Center for Nazarene Missionaries, located in Temple City,

California. During the week, Bob was in classes while weekends were filled with speaking engagements all over the California, Oregon districts and beyond.

We enjoyed being with my parents who returned from their assignment in Chile. Those were special family times, and meeting, sharing, and praying with the missionaries on Friday prayer times. Robin attended school that was close. It was a good season, both as a family and in friendship with the retired warriors of the faith.

I felt I belonged there, with my missionary family.

We also had the joy of visiting Bob's parents quite often. Freeman and Mildred, who lived in Grover Beach, California. We loved walking along Pismo Beach, wading in the cold water, and watching sunsets. Mildred was an excellent cook, and it was always a fun thing to ride up to Grover Beach for a visit.

It was during Bob's studies at Fuller, that we were able to go to Israel on a Studies program, offered to Old Testament students at Fuller. That was a wonderful trip. I felt that I was "on a honeymoon with Jesus". The Garden tomb, Bethlehem, the boat ride on the Sea of Galilee, and so many other beautiful and memorable sights. I felt greatly blessed by that trip, never knowing that our last assignment would be in the Middle East.

Wishing you God's blessings during the Christmas season and throughout the New Year.

Spurgeon & Fae Hendrix, with children, Arlan Ray and Norma Louise.

Buenos Aires, Argentina, circa 1947.

Home Assignment, Indian Lake, Michigan, 1949.

Home Assignment, Manchester, Indiana, 1949

Aunt Ruby, Mother's Sister and Norma.

Leon, Norma on family vacation, Cordoba, Argentina.

First Piano Recital, Buenos Aires, Argentina, 1951.

Piano, Buenos Aires, Argentina.

Hendrix Family, Coban, Oklahoma.

La Grande, Oregon, 1955.

Last picture taken in Cuba, 1960.

Back Row: Lucien Jones, Burnard Schmidt, Tony Mrotke, Jack Hoskins, J.D. Sharp, Mervin Hamman, Jim Mc Gill, C.H. Homer, Jim Burton, Louis Gill. 2nd. Row: Hazel Large, Norma Hendrix. 3rd. Row: John Showalter, Chief O.F. Mc Lain, Lester Longacre, Hubert Harris, Chester Longacre.

Police Department, Bethany, Oklahoma, 1962.

Wedding Day, Robert and Norma Brunson, November 24, 1964.

Bible School, Chiclayo, Peru.

Dr. Larry and Doris Fine.

Robert, Norma, Robin, Sheri Brunson, Costa Rica.

Students from SENDAS, Costa Rica, 1994.

Robert, Norma, Robin, Sheri, Olathe, Kansas 1998.

Mother, Ray, Leon and Norma, 2012.

Robert and Norma Brunson, Bradenton, 2018.

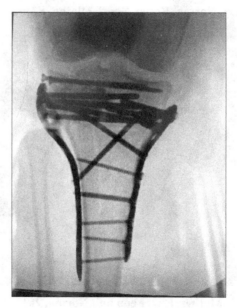

Broken Tibial Plateau, 2019

Standing tall and straight, 2021.

CHAPTER XIII

BELLA COSTA RICA- 1981

*W*e were surprised to find out that our next task was in Costa Rica, at the Seminary. Bob completed his Masters, and we celebrated his graduation with joy. Bob's parents, Freeman and Mildred, and my parents were able to join us for a great family time.

We packed for our new post. Bob's skill at carpentry was in full display as he made crates and one large one for my piano. He always amazed me at his expertise in wood-working. After retirement, I became enamored with his skill at wood carving, so beautifully detailed and perfect in dimension and size.

We quickly settled into our house in Guadalupe, a section of San Jose, the capital. We enrolled the girls in their schools and Bob set about getting his new assignment in order. He was at first the Dean of Students at the Seminary, as well as professor. I too was involved in teaching and helping with administrative duties.

Our arrival in Costa Rica occurred at a time when the Sandinista revolution was taking place. [1979-1990] There was an underlying sense of impending chaos and doom. Nicaraguans were fleeing and coming into Costa Rica. Propaganda against the United States was loud and daily on television and radio. Students at the Seminary were taking in much of the atmosphere. Tensions were underlying and felt. It was uncomfortable to daily hear the "Marxist rhetoric".

The splendor of Costa Rica spoke of God's creative genius, its breathtaking nature, and unrivaled beauty. However, for me personally, this decade ensued as a period of extreme darkness, frightening chaos, and gut-wrenching emotional pain. Bob and I were not communicating well. He seemed overwhelmed and tense most of the time. When Bob's father passed away, he left for California to attend the funeral. I felt angry that I could not go as well because I wanted to get away from the political and social tension. My life had become overcrowded with home life, seminary life, political anxiety and to crown it all, the ups and downs of menopause. I sensed I could not go on.

I was tired of trying to be a perfect missionary, a perfect wife, a perfect mother, a perfect Christian. I was tired. I was angry at the students who didn't understand the purposes of my heart. I couldn't change anything, and I felt burdened beyond belief. My prayer life was suffering. Anger and bitterness were taking root again in my spirit. My soul was infected with negativity and darkness. I was in trouble.

I began feeling more and more troubled. The dark hole was opening again. I was afraid. But I kept my thoughts to myself. I didn't feel I could confide in anyone.

BABY BOY

One day during these days of turmoil, my friend Julie, whose husband was head of World Vision for Central America, came to me with a request. She told me about a little boy that three years ago, at the age of one, swallowed lye and had burned his throat and esophagus. She added that he had been hospitalized for three years and a family in Nebraska wanted to adopt him. But until they came, she asked, "Norma would you mind taking care of him until they arrive? We want him to hear English so he's not so shocked when they take him home to the States."

I listened and responded. "Sure, I'll take him. For how long?" She said, "Three weeks". As I remember, I didn't pray about it. I asked Bob and he said yes. But I did have this thought, "If I take in this little Costa Rican boy, maybe they will know I'm a good American."

The day came for me to go to the hospital to bring him home. What I found was a thin, frail, and darling, little boy, sitting in a large baby crib. His big eyes looked up at me. The trachea in his neck told the story. His words were strained as he lifted his arms to be picked up. Julie lifted him and said, "This is your mommy for a few weeks." Immediately he looked at me and whispered, "Mama!" I held him and he held on tightly while Julie put his newly bought shoes on. He was ecstatic! He was smiling and pointing to the window. He was eager to get out! I learned that he weighed 17 pounds and was not potty trained. What I did not know, was what I was getting myself into.

From the start, he began to hold on to me as if saying, "Please don't take me back to the hospital". He would say, "Mama" and hug me and stroke my hair. He was endearing. But I soon found him to be quite manipulative. If he didn't like something, he threatened to pull out his stomach tube, which he did repeatedly. Several times, I had to rush him to the hospital so doctors could wash out his stomach hole, sterilize his stomach area and reinstate a new tube.

We found a cot that we placed for him in Sheri's room. I began the "potty training" process. I fully intended to care for him to the best of my ability. They informed me that I needed to cook his food, liquify it and then, using the pole, hang the feeding bottle upside down, hook his stomach tube to the bottle and sit with him while the food slowly dripped into his stomach. It took two hours, four times a day for the food to slowly drip. As I sat with him, I gave him cookies to chew on and then spit out into a bowl. At least that way he tasted sweet which he loved. It was grueling and necessary. I wanted to fatten him up, so I loaded his food with butter and cream, vegetables, chicken, pasta, and beef. My blender was working overtime! He soon began to fatten up.

He loved to play with Robin and Sheri. But he clung to me with persistence and jealousy. Many times, when one of the girls came up to me while I was holding him, he would say, "NO! My Mama!" and push them away.

One day, little Sheri, who was 4 years old at the time, came to me and said, "Mommy, when Carlitos leaves, am I leaving too?" My heart sank! I picked her up and held her tightly, "No honey! You are always mine and you will never leave. You are my daughter and I love you! We are just taking care of Carlitos for a time until his other parents come to get him." But that remark cut deep into my psyche. I felt angry that I had taken on Carlitos. The days were slowly become weeks. The strain was choking my sense of control. And I was losing it.

The long hours of sitting with him at mealtimes, plus the care for his trachea dragged on. On two different occasions, in the middle of the night, I was awakened, as if by the Lord, "Go check on Carlitos." I ran into his room and found him unable to breathe well. Mucous was blocking his trachea. I quickly pulled it out and cleaned it, rushing as I did so he could breathe. I never understood why the hospital didn't give me an aspirator. After both episodes, I could not sleep well for I was worried he would die if I didn't get there in time.

His stubbornness was taking its toll. He didn't want to wear his house shoes in the house, and we didn't want him to go barefooted on the damp tile floor. But he did. So, there was that battle with him, day in and day out. He wanted his shoes on only if he was going outside. Sometimes I felt that I wanted to rush him back to the hospital, but I knew

I couldn't. I was in a cage myself now. I was responsible to my friend Julie. I was responsible to the family who would be adopting him. I was responsible to Carlitos. I was responsible to my family. I was responsible to the church. I was responsible to the Seminary. And somewhere in there, I wanted my relationship with God. But it was all jumbled together in a pot of distress. And I wanted to fly away and forget it all.

After two long months, his adoptive parents came to Costa Rica to pick him up. They brought him a cute red, cowboy hat which he donned and loved. They were eager to take him. I suddenly was having separation anxiety of saying goodbye to this little boy, in whom I had invested all the love and care I could muster. I felt rewarded that at least he had gained ten pounds and was potty trained. And I thought that in some small way, he felt loved.

A friend drove Carlitos and me to the airport. Bob was teaching class and the girls were in school. We met at the airport terminal and walked into the building. Carlitos was safe in my arms and had no idea of how I was churning inside, with hurricanes, earthquakes, and tornadoes all at once.

We greeted them and I thanked them for their loving hearts and my best wishes for Carlitos. Then I said, "Carlitos, you get to ride on an airplane!" and I handed him over to his new mother. His arms instinctively came back towards me, and he yelled, "Mama! Mama!"

I motioned to them to quickly move on, and I said goodbye. I blindly walked to the waiting car and told my friend to drive me home. I was done and undone.

"Let's take a break today", he said." I want you to pick up tomorrow where you left off. I want you to try to recall all the emotions you were feeling during this period. It will help us see some patterns."

I was frankly sick of my life and retelling it was tiring. I had little emotional strength left.

CHAPTER XIV

BATTLE FOR MY SOUL

The day I dropped off Carlitos into his adoptive parents' arms, I knew I was going to walk away. When I got home, my friend Dora, had arrived to help with household chores and be present when Robin and Sheri got home. I told her that I was going for a walk. I wrote Bob a note saying: "I've had it. I can't take anymore. I love you. But I'm gone. Love, Norma."

I picked up a large bag. Added my billfold and two more things, my makeup kit, and my Bible.

Interesting couple of items there. Do you know why you picked those three things?

He irritated me with his interruptions. I tried to answer calmly, "Well, I like to look my best, and my mother always told me to take my Bible whenever I went away on a trip. So, I guess that's why."

He smiled. Waited. I guessed he wanted me to go on.

I donned my most comfortable sandals and walked out the door. It was about 9 o'clock in the morning. I walked for hours. I wore bleeding blisters on my feet. I kept walking, down hills, up hills in the Guadalupe area of San Jose. During the last few months, I had lost weight and was down to 120 lbs. I was getting tired.

When I saw the Catholic Church in Guadalupe, I walked in, took a seat at the back, and watched the crowds. Some walked up to a statue of Mary and prayed. Others sat down and worshipped. Others knelt at the kneeling benches for prayer. It suddenly struck me, "Norma, you came to Costa Rica to help people find God and here you are, worse off than they."

I saw myself as the prodigal daughter, confused and lost. I felt I was far from my Father's House. I got up and approached the phone booth. Whom could I call? Who would help me?

Rev. Phil Truesdale was pastor of the Union Church in Costa Rica and he and his wife, Marjorie, were friends of ours. I called Phil, "I need to talk to you. Would you pick me up at the Guadalupe Catholic Church?" He said yes.

They came and took me to their home. I began sharing my confusion and exhaustion. I told them that I was in deep emotional trouble and wanted to run away. I needed help. I said, "I don't want Bob to know." They listened but said, "We need to tell Bob. You are safe with us, but we need to tell Bob." Which they did.

I went to a bedroom in their house and fell asleep. I slept for hours. I don't know when I woke up, but Bob was there when I did. We talked and then went home. Bob wanted to connect and talk. But I didn't want to. All I wanted to do was run away. I didn't belong anywhere, but I didn't know to whom and where to go. All I understood was that my soul was dry, my emotions spent. I didn't have anything with which to care for anyone, husband, children, other people, or myself.

My mind is foggy as I recall those days. I do remember that Bob planned a beach trip for just the two of us. We left the girls with Dora and drove to Jaco Beach. I was unhappy. I was separated from myself, from Bob, from God and family. I didn't understand myself and I didn't want help. I just wanted out.

We stayed for two days, but I kept telling Bob that I wanted to go home. So, we packed up and he went to pay the bill. I walked out and started walking down the road. I really wanted to walk out into the ocean and keep walking, but I hurried down the road as fast and as far away as I could. Soon, I heard a car behind me. It was Bob. He said, "Norma, get in the car." I knew I had to. We drove back to San Jose. He held my hand the entire time. He told me later that he was afraid that I would open the door and jump out. I hadn't thought of that one!

When we arrived home, I asked him to call the doctor to give me a shot to put me out. He did and I slept for two days straight. When I came to, I told Bob that I wanted to go to the Kansas City and sign myself into a psych ward and see what was going on with me. Two days later Bob, the girls and I were headed to Kansas City on the next plane out. We arrived at the psych ward at 10:00 p.m. I walked in and said, "I need help". They signed me in, and I said good-bye to Bob and the girls.

The session ended and he told me he would soon talk to me about some of his diagnosis and plan of treatment. He added, "I do want to tell you, that I suspect your religion is a large part of your problem."

Nothing out of that man's mouth would have shocked me more 'My religion?' I figured out right then and there that he was going to be of no help to me at all. Little did I know.

The next couple of days were spent having group and counselor meetings, meals and talking to other patients. Then one day the nurse told me to go to the psychiatrist's office.

I sat down. "First of all, we believe you are manic-depressive and need to take medication. Secondly, as I told you, we believe your religion is one of your problems."

After hearing those two diagnoses, I was close to the first tears I had shed in a long time. He asked me, "Do you have any questions?" I said, "No, not really". He immediately prescribed Lithium. I fought the idea and cried myself to sleep that night, so afraid that I was utterly losing my mind and now with medication, would be a druggie forever.

I left his office but held back the tears. My next meeting was music therapy. It was our practice to go in and choose a song title that depicts one's mood or feelings for the day. I was late to my meeting but went anyway. When I walked in, I burst into tears. There was a group of about eight people in the room. They all crowded around me and began embracing and holding me while I sobbed and sobbed. Between loud and excruciating tears, I blubbered our, "I'm manic-depressive!" and more tears and sobs. More embraces and just hugs.

One of the lasting impressions of that moment is this; rather than judge me, they embraced my weakness, my limitation, my illness, my shame, my fear and accepted me. They could because they too, were weak, and limited, and ill and filled with fear and shame. And they understood me. And cared for me the best they could.

Years later, I understood one big truth God was teaching me. Bob and I used the hymn on our deputation slides' theme song, "Sinner Saved by Grace". We are all in need of His saving Grace until the day we die and meet Him. None of us is free to judge or condemn. Because, we too have been sinful in need of a Savior. Big spiritual truth learned in a psyche ward.

Beside the psychiatrist, each patient had a counselor. I liked mine. He was a gentle young man who listened, guided my thoughts towards self-analysis and I felt a comfortable bond with him. One day they told me that I was going to have another counselor. I asked why. They told me that the previous counselor was feeling he was getting too attached to me. He needed to be professional and knew when it was moving past counselor-patient to something more. I was angry with him because I felt he really understood me. Later, I deeply appreciated his honesty because I was very vulnerable, and he knew it.

The Lithium was closing off my brain. I could barely finish one sentence. I couldn't think clearly, and I was taking less than the prescribed dosage. I hated feeling slow. I detested the struggle to finish a sentence. The counseling sessions were useless as far as I was concerned. I was existing in a safe place. I was broken and hurting. But I also knew I wanted to go home.

The only person I wanted to see was my brother Ray. He was the only one that didn't ask anything from me. I felt badly for Bob. He was at his wits ends with me. Yet we knew that he and I had a lot of work to do to learn how to live anew after my emotional break. I felt very guilty for what I was doing to my family. My parents had retired and had come to Kansas City to visit Ray and Claire. When I told my mother that I didn't want to see her, she was crushed. But at this time, I had to take care of me.

Every day I went through the routine of counseling session, occupational, group, and music therapies. I endured occupational, but soon realized that if I wanted to get out of the psyche ward, I was going to have to comply. I spent Christmas in the Psyche Ward. I didn't have to care for anyone, cook meals, decorate, or entertain. I was free to do as I pleased. I was hospitalized for five weeks and finally given permission to go home to Ray and Claire's house where Bob and the girls were staying. I felt like a walking zombie.

CHAPTER XV

BATTLING ON THREE FRONTS

*B*ob rented a duplex in Olathe, Kansas. I had lost more weight and Bob bought me some lovely clothes at Macy's. The day arrived to take me home. He was holding down three jobs and I knew he was struggling to hold our family together. But I couldn't take care of him at this time. My days were filled with doctor's appointments, counseling sessions, rest, and spending time at my brother's house. Robin and Sheri were in school.

One day, I told Bob. I want to do something that will mark this time in my life. I want to get my ears pierced. He was appalled but he said, "Okay." I remember thinking as he took me to the Claire's Store for the big event, "This is the first time I have gone against my mother's wishes." I still wear and do not remove two small diamonds earrings that Bob gave me several years ago.

I hadn't been home for just a few weeks when I noticed that I was having trouble walking to and from the bathroom. I felt weak and it took me forever to just dress myself. A few days later my brother stated that I looked jaundiced. Bob took me to the doctor who informed me that I had Hepatitis A and needed complete bed rest. Those were the darkest days yet. I was depleted emotionally and sick physically. My spiritual life on hold.

My blurred mind and inability to complete sentences was bothering me. So, I decided to go off Lithium cold turkey. I did not tell my psychiatrist. One night, I was awakened by a dark, ominous presence in my room. It seemed like Satan himself was to appear at the foot of my bed. I had a tape player by my bed, and I quietly rolled over and turned it on. Bob woke up and asked me, "Having a hard time, Norma?" I said, "Yes, it's awful!" I turned off the music and got up.

I don't' think I had been into reading the Bible for quite a while because I hadn't been able to concentrate. But that night, with fear gripping my very soul, I picked up my Bible, closed the bedroom door and went into the kitchen. I was feeble but determined to get relief. I spoke out loud, "God, I have had enough. I feel Satan is about to drag me down for good. So, tonight, I'm not going back to bed until you give me a scripture to hold on to." I walked back and forth reading the Psalms. Back and forth and forth and back. Reading out loud. In my weakened condition, I doggedly persevered. It was grit and guts, but I was desperate.

"Surely he will save you from the fowler's snare and from the deadly pestilence. He will cover you with his feathers, and under his wings you will find refuge; his faithfulness will be your shield and rampart. You will not fear the terror of night nor the arrow that flies by day, nor the pestilence that stalks in the darkness." Psalm 91:3-6a

It was if a beam of incredible brightness broke into the dark hole in my soul. Suddenly I felt the terror dissipate. Exhausted, but peaceful, I returned to my bed and slept for hours. The light had begun to shine, now I had to find the path.

My brother Ray and wife Claire, the Olathe College Church family and personal friends were among my support during that time. My parents finally came to visit, and I was able to embrace them and explain some of the turmoil I was experiencing.

One day, my college friend, Doris Fine came to visit. She had been in our wedding, and I was so grateful for her kind and loving words of encouragement. She asked me if I would be willing to seek some help from her husband.

Dr. Larry Fine was professor of Practical Theology at Mid America Nazarene University in Olathe, Kansas. At that time, he had just completed three years working in a mental health facility as well carrying his teaching load. I knew Larry from college days. He and Bob were in the same graduating class and Doris was one year ahead of me. I agreed and she said she would ask Larry if it fit into his schedule. She got back to me, and they set up evening counseling times.

I went to my first visit. I was glad to see Doris sitting at a desk outside Larry's office. I felt safe seeing her soft smile.

CHAPTER XVI

BLURTING AND BABBLING

*L*arry invited me to sit down. He sat across from me. He asked me what was going on. I wondered where to start. At first slowly and hesitantly I told him the first layer. "

"Life is too hard," I said.

"Tell me more."

"I just don't want to go on living like this." He looked at me intently and asked if I had thought about taking my life.

"No, I wouldn't do that. But I know why people kill themselves. When the hole is so deep and so dark, and no way out, one thinks about it."

"One, or you?"

"Well, I think about how to exist in the hole, I guess. And I hate it."

I felt myself relax and I kept on talking. Once I started, I couldn't stop. I spewed on and on, reliving, retelling, repeating, recounting, rehearsing. I was getting sicker and sicker of hearing me share all the pain, the hurts the stuff. I didn't realize he was too.

I rambled, "My mother did this to me. I got too many spankings. My father didn't know what to do with me. The missionaries were unfair to us. My husband this and my husband that. The church was unfair to us. My friends hurt me. I worked hard and no one understands. I love God but He's not close to me I've worked hard, and it seems for naught. I just want to quit."

He spoke. *"You signed yourself into a psych ward. You've agreed to come to me for help. I think the last thing you want to do is quit. But let's get something straight right away. If we are going on a pity party here, I want you to know I am terribly busy. I don't have time and you don't have it either. But, if you want to work on some deeper issues, I'm here for you. So, let's start again."*

I looked at him with darts of anger. They didn't faze him. I had met my match. I soon realized I could not control, connive, or deceive him. I wanted to walk out, but he brought me back and spoke gently,

"Norma, I'm here to work with you on YOU, not anyone else. I am here to walk with you, to look with you at your

inner self, and perhaps help you discover the real Norma, the Norma that God created, beautifully and uniquely."

I started to cry. And I couldn't stop. He sat there, handed me Kleenex, and let me cry. My first session was over. He said, "I look forward to our next time." I wondered if I could stand his piercing discernment.

BECOMING VULNERABLE

"When I think of my childhood, I feel...?" he asked.

I knew my parents loved God first and us children, secondly. I never doubted that. Yet it seemed that everyone was more important than we. It was as if we were so loved and cared for, that we had all we needed. But other people were more needy, and my parents were always trying to meet somebody's need. We had orphans, widows, politician's daughters, and others in our home, in and out constantly.

"I have felt so many times," I continued, "That I wasn't allowed to breathe, that I was taking someone else's air or that I was standing in someone else's place on the floor. I truly have felt the need to ask forgiveness for my existence."

I added, "Somehow I seemed to be basically wrong – not right. Why would my godly parents spank me so much if I wasn't terribly 'not right?' Why would my father say so many times, 'Oh, Norma, I don't know what to do with you!' A grown man, couldn't handle me? So, I prayed at the

117

altar more. I tried harder. 'If I do more, I'll be acceptable to God and my parents. 'The inner battles of trying hard to live up to others' expectations is exhausting."

I told him that my parents worked all the time. They seemed stressed all the time. They had problems in the church, or the Bible School, and they seemed to always be solving problems. They had multiple responsibilities and at night, after tucking us in bed, walked the four city blocks the Bible School that stood at 884 Donato Alvarez Avenue. I remember hating it when they left us. Nata was in her room, and we were supposed to stay in bed. I didn't like the quiet house. I think I felt scared.

"What would you tell your mother, if you could, Norma?"

I thought long and hard. I knew my mother's own life was ruggedly painful. She didn't have a good role model. I knew she and my father loved me and did their best. But now, I needed to receive inner belonging. I needed to confess the feelings of distrust and fear that I had even towards God.

Slowly I began to face my inner self with honesty and in the presence of the Holy Spirit. I learned that God is pleased with us when we are honest before Him. I discovered that His Shoulders are broad enough to handle my stuff. I soon was able to move forward into forgiveness and freedom. I confessed my experience with truth to God Himself as we prayed together.

I shared that I perceived early on that life was a struggle. That the only way through was to pray and work hard, work hard, and pray. Somehow, I grew to believe the lie that God likes busy people.

My concept of God was rigid, as if He were always waiting to show me how wrong I am. His Love seemed so distant from my reality. But slowly, I began to feel freedom from the straitjacket of legalism. "It is by Grace that we have been saved, through faith – and this not from yourselves, it is the gift of God." [Ephesians 2:8]

Larry helped me move from "Works" to "Grace". He emphasized the importance of studying the book of Ephesians. He asked me to go through the book carefully and see "Who We Are and What We Have in Christ". He allowed me to experience God's forgiveness as we looked at the compassion Jesus had for those needing healing, forgiveness, and hope.

Another great truth Larry brought out was the importance of seeking God's truth against Satan's lies. *"Is that a lie, Norma?" What does God's Word say about that?"*

One day I remembered the psychiatrist's words,

"We believe your religion is part of your problem."

I realized that he didn't really know what he meant but I now did! And he was right! I had some basics really screwed up! And now I was moving from "Rigid Religion" to "Rebirth and Renewal", all by the Grace of Jesus Christ through His Holy Spirit at work in me.

There were many sessions more. I began to sense freedom and trust in God. I forgave and loved my parents more than ever. I continued the forgiveness path that I had started years before at our apartment in Nashville. God was gracious in accepting my confession. And I thank Larry and Doris Fine for being my safe brother and sister in Christ, who helped me gain spiritual strength and footing in the Love and Grace of our Lord Jesus.

Larry was a working with FOCUS, a Kansas City-established personal-effectiveness conference. I was able to attend and developed my own personal statement which I carry in my billfold to this day. It reminds me of who I am in Christ.

The scripture, "Confess your sins, one to another." [James 5:16] gives us permission to confess, our private issues, sins, or damaged emotions. I believe we, as the body of Christ, would find help and comfort if we quickly acknowledged areas in our personal lives that need the Holy Spirit's healing. I was glad I had someone with whom I could share my struggles. It was humbling, but very necessary.

CHAPTER XVII

BOUND FOR CHICAGO-
August 1983

$\mathscr{B}$ ob received an invitation from the Chicago Central Church of the Nazarene to become Director of the Ethnic-Urban Ministries for the Chicago Thrust to the Cities Emphasis. We moved to Chicago, and settled in a lovely home in Elmhurst, Illinois. The girls' school was nearby, and Bob drove daily to his office in downtown Chicago.

Those were years of quiet healing for me. I was glad that Bob had his ministry and for the first time, I was able to be home and grow emotionally and spiritually in unhindered ways. Slowly my strength was returning. Kay Young and I began team teaching a Sunday School Class at Chicago First Church of the Nazarene. We made lasting friendships in our years there.

I was finally able to work part-time and found receptionist's job at Elmhurst Clinic. That continued to help heal my Spirit as I moved out into the working world and learned new skills of connecting. I always had the phone to call Larry and Doris if I needed a reminder of lessons learned in Larry's office.

During the Chicago years, Bob and I made some clear-cut decisions about our relationship. We talked openly and honestly about our struggles. I knew Bob was eager to learn and so was I. At times Bob and I called Larry and asked for advice. He guided us in the art of listening to one another, openly and actively. God knew our hearts and we loved each other despite our quite different approaches to problem solving. We learned to solve problems creatively and calmly. I learned to face issues without attacking the problem full force but allowed the other to process. Bob needed time to think things through. My impetuousness led him to panic. We both learned to adjust to the other and as result grew in our respect, acceptance, and love for one another.

BELIEVE IT OR NOT! – December 1987

We received a letter from the Department of World Mission asking if we would be willing to return to Costa Rica and the Seminary! Bob's eyes filled with tears. Teaching was his first love! We embraced and danced and thanked God! We felt that was where we truly belonged.

Our assignment was to the Seminario Nazareno de Las Americas, [SENDAS] in San Jose. Bob continued teaching his classes in Theology, Old Testament, and Christian

Beliefs. He translated a Hebrew textbook from English/ Hebrew into Spanish. I was so proud of the hard work he invested in teaching Hebrew and Greek as well as his other responsibilities.

My duties were Director of Public Relations/Work and Witness. It was a privilege to serve the Lord with the volunteer teams that came to Costa Rica to help build the needed buildings on campus. One of my joys was working with a singing group, called AMELAC. Their genre was Andean Music. We organized a trip to the General Assembly to sing and travel 6,000 miles in the United States ministering in many churches.

One of the highlights for Work and Witness Team members was our bus ride to visit the Poas Volcano. On one of those trips, I met I met two couples, who were American doctors and their wives. They were visiting Costa Rica and had biked up to the volcano from San Jose and were getting ready to bike back.

It was a beautiful day. When our time was up, we headed down the mountain back towards the city. As we rounded a bend, I noticed a group of people by the side of the road. As we drew closer, I saw one of the doctors kneeling over someone. I told the bus driver to stop. I got off and there, bleeding profusely was one of the men I had just met up at the top. He had slipped on gravel and his bike careened off the road. He hit a huge rock and his head was busted wide open. I was the only one there that could speak Spanish to the onlookers. I asked for privacy, and I was able to steer people away to talk to the crying friend. The women were both standing up the driveway close to a coffee shop.

The doctor friend was in tears. "We served together in Viet Nam and made it through that war to come here and see him die like this?" It was heart rending. I felt I needed to help. I was able to meet them later at their hotel and pray with them. I offered all the assistance I could to get the body shipped to the States. They were open to comfort and help. Something touched my heart in a prophetic way, "Someday, I want to be a chaplain."

During this time, I was able to complete an MA in Human Resource Management/Counseling from Azusa Pacific University in California. My dissertation title was: "A Biblical, Psychological, Historical Case Study of Demonic Contamination, Oppression and Possession." I took four case studies of people with whom I had inter- acted that showed, what I believed to be signs of demonic activity. It took three years to complete the study. I was glad to be done with it. I learned much.

Our furlough coincided with graduation, and I was able to walk through the graduating line with my peers. I was so glad my parents were able to be with Bob and me for that special day, July 31, 1993.

BYE-BYE ROBIN!

Robin's graduation from High School in Costa Rica, was a beautiful reminder of all the years we had the privilege of having our family together. We also knew that she was preparing to study at Southern Nazarene University. I dreaded that day, but it did arrive. We reminded Robin that she was following a family tradition as we photographed my father, Robin, and Norma in front of the university sign. We helped Robin moved into her dorm room. We stayed a couple of days and then headed back to Costa Rica.

I knew what my mother felt when, back in 1962, she and my father left me in Bethany as they returned to Argentina. Bob and I were so proud of Robin. She had taken a stand for God and was determined to serve Him. She had been compliant and obedient, yet she had determination and a strong will. I knew that once she decided to "follow Jesus", nothing could stop her. I trusted her as much as I cried for miles knowing how much I would miss my Robin.

CHAPTER XVIII

BOUND FOR HOME ASSIGNMENT

*W*e enjoyed our work in Costa Rica and felt that God used us according to our gifts. But he also gave us some creativity in presenting the missionary story on furlough. We always had a "woman" that exemplified a country we represented, that in some and unusual way came to faith in Jesus Christ.

Our custom was for us to go to the church and meet the pastor. Then I hid in some room where I changed into my "typical" dress and waited for my cue to enter the sanctuary. Oh, I could write a book on those experiences alone! I always wore a hat or a head scarf, depending on the country I was representing.

When Bob got up to preach, I walked in and sat near the back. Of course, I always looked "different" if not strange. People turned around and looked and I tended to put my head down in "embarrassment" until Bob's cue to say,

"My, I think a friend of mine just walked into this church! And I would love for you to meet her!" Then he started the pulling and tugging to try to get me up on the platform to "meet and be met" by the congregation. I used an accent, either from Latin America or from the Middle East depending on my garb. And we had fun bantering back and forth. One line I pulled on Bob, simply threw him and the crowd into roars of laughter. I asked him, "You Mr. Brunson, yes?" He nodded and said, "Yes, yes." "Mr. Brunson, you the man with the beautiful wife?" Roar and laughter and Bob was speechless. I started using that line and it worked!

In one church, the grouchy-looking saint of God, looked at me as I sat down. She said, "The least you could do is take your hat off in church!" Well, I didn't. Another lady was so kind and compassionate. When I acted as though I was embarrassed and didn't want to go up to "meet the missionary", she leaned over with all the love and care in the world and said, "Go ahead, honey, he won't hurt you!" That was one place and time that I laughed all the way through the presentation. Bob did too. It was tough going trying to stifle laughter while telling the good news story!

I felt God really used the method and the message to touch hearts and I give him all the glory! Many times, I slipped out, after we finished and during the offering would occasionally hear, "Where is that lady that gave her testimony?" I smiled and said, "Well, that would be me!" And they added, "Oh you don't always talk like that?" It was

fun and it was effective, and I smile as I remember deputation. It was a privilege to serve the Lord overseas and at
home as well.

I clearly see that one place I felt I belonged was on stage,
acting out some character, in which I could lose myself.

BOUND FOR TRINITY EVANGELICAL
DIVINITY SCHOOL

Bob had been accepted at Trinity Evangelical Divinity
School to begin working on his PHD in Old Testament.
Those were two incredibly stressful years. Bob studied
all week and on Fridays, Bob, Norma, and Sheri took off
on Southwest Airlines for a Faith Promise or Missionary
service somewhere. The flights home, late at night, were
excruciating! We were so tired! I knew Bob was trying
to finish his studies and keep up the routine of speaking
engagements all over the United States.

It was a wild ride. We lived in a small apartment. Sheri
was in Junior High and Robin in college. During one of
those years, Robin took a missionary assignment in New
Zealand, so we didn't see her for one year.

I knew Bob was struggling with his health. And it took
its toll. We rushed him to the hospital with a heart attack.
He had stents inserted and was told to take it easy. That
was hard to do. Soon we were back in the routine, running,
doing, going, coming. What a rat race! The second year I

took a teaching job at a nearby elementary school. That helped with finances.

When Bob completed his course work, we returned to Costa Rica and the Seminary. We drove from Chicago all the way to Costa Rica. It took us eleven days, driving only during the day. Our travels through Mexico, and Central America were a delight. Sheri kept a diary and that would be another epistle! When we arrived in early December, we enrolled Sheri in the 9th grade at Marian Baker School and moved into my favorite home of all time. It was December 1994.

BUT WE JUST GOT HERE!

In June 1995, a meeting was called at the Seminary with the leaders from Headquarters. Dr. Louie Bustle met with all of us to inform that the Seminary would be closing. All missionary staff would be re-deployed. We looked at one another in shock and disbelief. We just got here!

Dr. Bustle offered to send us either to Argentina or to the Seminary in Switzerland. We felt we needed to pray about it and consider our family situation. Sheri had just entered High School and Bob needed to complete his PHD. So, after prayer and consideration, we opted to return to the United States.

CHAPTER XIX

BACK TO THE UNITED STATES

$\mathcal{W}$e moved into a duplex in Stilwell, KS. Sheri enrolled at Blue Valley High School. And Bob soon received an offer to serve as pastor the Kansas City Kansas Spanish Church of the Nazarene. One day a surprising offer fell into my hands; enroll in the Clinical Pastoral Education Course at Baptist Medical Center in Kansas City Missouri. I remembered the Poas Volcano, the bike riders, the moment a desire swelled up in my heart. And here was my chance.

I must interject some of the family issues we were facing. I knew Sheri was unhappy and I understood why. She, as I, so many times, felt displaced, out of her element in the States. But in Peru or Costa Rica, she blended in. She was Hispanic.

However, she remarked how people in the United States made derogatory remarks. She started working at Penny's. One day she overheard a lady say, "She speaks pretty good English for a Mexican!" My heart hurt for Sheri. She was struggling with this new environment, and she missed Costa Rica. I understood her need to belong. And I knew she felt she didn't. There were some difficult days.

BLAZING NEW TRAILS

I must admit I was unprepared for CPE. But since I was headed towards my dream, I had to go through the training. My first encounter with my supervisor was shocking. He did not speak to me. He avoided me. In groups, he spoke with others and dismissed anything I said. We had group meetings and in one of those sessions, we all received a name. My name was Bulldozer. And that said it all.

The intensity of self-awareness is key to learning the art of "other" awareness. I soon realized I had much to learn. I discovered ways in which I manipulated the conversations to head in the direction I desired. It was made clear to me that I was controlling and pushy. In all honesty, I was unaware of these qualities in my character. It was a humbling, but necessary path of personal development, and I am so grateful for the lessons of "self" I learned in CPE.

My training took 55 hours a week for one year and a half. I was on call one night a week, covering all areas and wards of the hospital. The group sessions were rich in self-awareness. It took introspection and honesty to wade through one's personal biases and preferences. The goal was to see how those issues impede one's ability to truly be present in the life of another. I completed my training having finished six CPE units.

Concurrent with my intense CPE training, I was also completing the course of study necessary for Ordination. I felt joy and humble gratitude the night General Superintendent Dr. James Diehl ordained me as Elder in the Church of the Nazarene. It was August 15, 1996, at Olathe College Church of the Nazarene. After meeting the Board of Chaplain Ministries for the Church of the Nazarene, I received my Ecclesiastical Endorsement as Chaplain on September 18, 1996. My Costa Rican Poas dream had come true.

BECOMING A COLLEGE PROFESSOR- 1997

While Bob was blazing his own "trail" as pastor of the Spanish congregation, and working on his doctoral studies, I received an invitation to teach Spanish at Mid America Nazarene University in Olathe, KS. The present Chair and Spanish Professor was taking three years off to complete her doctoral studies. I felt honored to get into the classroom. I divided my time between the Spanish curriculum during the day and the Adult Education Program in the evenings, teaching courses related to Human Resource Management.

Those were incredibly full years, both professionally and personally. Our daughters both faced new epochs in their lives. I enjoyed helping Robin prepare for her wedding to Carlos Radziszewski on June 13, 1998. His father, Bruno and Bob performed the wedding ceremony in Shawnee Church of the Nazarene.

We also welcomed Sheri's new daughter, Lindsey Fae Brunson into the world. Sheri and Lindsey came to live with us until Lindsey was 18 months old. She was a beautiful baby, sweet and easy to care for. I loved holding my first grandchild and seeing her grow, develop and learn.

The years between 1997 and 2000 would take another epistle!

BYE-BYE DADDY!

It was during this time, that my father and mother lived at Casa Robles, in Temple City. My mother called me one day to tell me that daddy wasn't doing well. My brothers and I met in California. My father had suffered the effects of Alzheimer's for about ten years. Now he couldn't swallow. He had been catatonic for several years, not speaking or relating. So, I knew that his time was short.

We met with the doctors, and all agreed that he was being placed on DO NOT RESUSCITATE. That was his wish.

Before I left to return to Kansas City, I went one more time to the hospital to tell him goodbye. He was lying in the bed, mouth open and eyes closed. Suddenly he opened his eyes, looked at the television that was showing the Lucy show. He started giggling and said, "They are funny!" and then looked at me and spoke, first time in two or three years, "Hi girlie! I love you!" and he pursed his lips to kiss me. "I love you daddy!" and I kissed him. That was the last thing he said. I felt so blessed. I love my daddy and miss him. He passed away in December of 1996.

BETWIXED AND BETWEEN

I had completed all the requirements necessary to be hired as Hospital Chaplain and was in the process of becoming Board Certified Clinical Hospital Chaplain when I received a call. My supervisor, Dr. Jim Harper, asked if I would be willing to take the lead position as Chaplain at Menorah Medical Center in Overland, Park, Kansas. I told him I would pray about it.

Bob and I prayed for several days. I wasn't sure and we needed "Heavenly Clearance". In the middle of our seeking answers, we received a call from Dr. Louie Bustle. He explained that the Gordon Johnstons were soon retiring from their service in the Middle East. "Would we be willing to go to Lebanon for Bob to serve as Director of the Eastern Mediterranean Nazarene Bible College."

Bob and I looked at each other, "The Middle East"? We prayed. We knew. We said Yes. I called Jim Harper and thanked him but stated that our assignment with our church took precedence. We packed up. Said good-byes and landed in Beirut, Lebanon one November day in 2000.

CHAPTER XX

BEIRUT

$\mathcal{G}$ ordon Johnston rented an apartment for us looking out over Cedars of Lebanon and the Mediterranean Sea. I repeatedly scratched my head in disbelief. "What was I doing here?" Yet I knew that God had sent us.

The Middle Eastern Culture is beautiful in its hospitality. We suddenly felt welcomed by the church family. Brother Abdo, Marlene, Raja, Seta, all made our entry into this new culture easy. We slowly learned some of the innuendos of this new world. Dr. Habib gave us a lesson in Cultural Awareness and showed us the varying degrees of meanings in body language, hospitality customs and boundaries. He not only took care of our physical needs, but he helped us adjust with a deeper understanding of our new environment.

We enrolled in Language Study and began the arduous task of learning the phonetic sounds of Arabic. Our teacher was charming and kind. The language was brutal! But we struggled on. I had my church friends laughing when I spoke Arabic with my "foreign accent".

Bob became acquainted with the details of EMNBC. We found out that the professors travel to the students [Syria, Jordan, and the Holy Land] and once a year, all students meet at the hotel in Jerash, Jordan for one month of intensives. That became a wonderful time of bonding. Our friends were owners of the hotel in Jerash, and we found our Muslim friends open and friendly to us. We felt privileged to be invited to their daughter's wedding in Jerash.

Bob and I both traveled throughout the countries teaching varying courses. Although most students knew English, most classes were taught through an interpreter. I taught two courses in Jordan. One was in Irbid. At that time, Irbid was known to have more Internet Cafés than any other city in the world. Well, who knew if that was right? However, I will attest to it having many!

My classes were at night. My host and hostess were the pastors of the Irbid Church of the Nazarene. Both were out of the house most of the day, so I "walked the streets" during the day, going to stores, getting on the internet, and learning the culture in this University town. I was appalled to find that porn came up first on every computer in every internet café that I opened. My heart was heavy to see the proliferation of the darkness and innate selfishness of that vice.

It was evident that I was not a Muslim as I walked the streets. Both men and women who are Christians in the

Middle East, tend to wear a cross as a necklace. I also did not cover my head. I remember facing a man in the street who was saying crude things to me. In my broken Arabic I faced him and said, "I could be your mother! Stop with the vulgarities!" Oh my! I learned so much!

I traveled by myself by bus to Damascus, Syria to teach a course. Damascus is said to be the oldest continuously inhabited city in the world. The Nazarene Church is in the old part of Damascus, just a few blocks from Straight Street, famous for being part of the Apostle Paul's conversion story. There were about 15 students present.

The pastor of the church came in and whispered to me in English, "Don't read the syllabus yet. Just talk lightly about any subject. We have a government official here." So, we began chatting about ways to show care and love to each other. We talked on and on, bantering and preparing to "teach". Finally, it was break time. After coffee, the pastor told me, "He's gone. You can read the syllabus now." We were able to teach the course on Christian Beliefs without any more interruptions. I loved their hearts and desire for learning. Church services were incredible times of spiritual bonding. Their hunger for God in the face of growing opposition moved my heart to a closer walk with God.

While in Damascus, I stumbled over a cobblestone in the road and fell hard on my right shoulder! Oh my! The Pain! I figured if Paul had fallen to the ground not far from here, I could too! The neighbors came out of their homes offering me help, a chair to sit on and called a taxi to take me to the nearest doctor for an Xray. It showed a broken shoulder! He gave me a shot of pain killer and I boarded a taxi for my ride back to Beirut. The driver was so kind as we rode over bumps in the road. He kept saying, "I'm so sorry, Madam! So Sorry!"

Dr. Habib and Bob met me at the hospital, and he set my arm against my chest for a month, waiting for my shoulder to heal. I learned to write with my left hand during that month!

BABY GRANDDAUGHTER!

Robin and Carlos were on home assignment in Kansas City. Robin was expecting her first child born, August 31, 2001. I received permission to travel to Kansas City for two weeks to be with Robin and Carlos and welcome my new Grandbaby Nicol! I was also able to be with Sheri and her family.

I woke up on Tuesday morning, September 11, made some coffee and walked into the living room. The house was still quiet. I turned on the television, just as a second plane flew into the World Trade Center.

I called Bob in Beirut to let him know what was happening. He too had heard. The next few days we stayed glued to the television. But my two-weeks were nearing an end and I knew I had to get back to Bob and Beirut.

I called headquarters and was told that as soon as I could, I should head back to Lebanon. I'll never forget the wonderful friend and General Superintendent Talmadge Johnson who called me, "Norma, I want to know when you board the plane and when you arrive in Lebanon. I will be praying for you the entire time." I said good-bye to my family in Kansas City with tears and boarded a plane for Lebanon. How ironic that I was taking a plane back home to the area from which the idea of smashing planes into buildings originated!

Bob and our friends met me at the airport. It was good to get that safe hug from Bob. I didn't ever want to be separated from him again, especially in the Middle East. Our friends offered their sorrowful condolences for what happened to my country. I thanked God for the safe trip. I called Dr. Johnson and let him know how much I appreciated his concern for my welfare.

BAD NEWS! IRAQ WAR! 2003

Our denomination owned a home on the island of Cypress where in years past, EMNBC students met to take the summer intensives. As news of impending war in Iraq was filling the news waves, we received orders from our headquarters to evacuate to Cypress. So, In the early part of March 2003, missionaries Rod Green, Philip Rodebush [both serving in Jordan] and Bob and Norma, met in Cypress and waited out for about six weeks until Headquarters felt it was safe for us to return to our separate countries.

We taught courses continuously, in Lebanon, Syria and Jordan. During this time, I was working on my MA in Theology from Manchester University and through the Nazarene Theological College. I thoroughly enjoyed the three-weeks of intensives held once a year. I learned about Pauline's Theology on Sanctification. My dissertation's title was, "A Pauline Paradigm for Women in Ministry: Nazarene Women in the Middle East." It was approved and in October of 2005, I traveled to Manchester, England to graduate with a MA of Arts in Theology.

CHAPTER XXI

BEIRUT AND THE AMERICAN
EMBASSY-December 2005

*T*he phone rang in our apartment. The woman's voice, "This is J. from the American Embassy here in Beirut, may I speak to Norma Louise Brunson?"

"This is she," I responded.

She continued, "Please come to the embassy immediately. Take side roads and I'll be waiting for you. Do you know a Robert Brunson?"

"Yes, he's my husband." She added, "Bring him with you".

I asked, "Is this for all Americans?"

"Just come as soon as possible." And she hung up.

We quickly got into our car and drove the 10 miles across Beirut to the 17-acre embassy compound. It sat high on a hill, overlooking the Mediterranean. We walked past machine-gun-carrying guards, through security and into a patio. A black car was waiting for us. A man stepped out and said, "Mr. and Mrs. Brunson?" Bob said, "yes".

"Please get in."

He drove us over two metal barriers that closed back up behind us and into the back part of the compound. We got out and walked into a building with J. waiting for us. She led us to a back room where the attaché for Security met us. He asked if we wanted anything to drink. We said no.

He called and asked his secretary to hold all calls. He closed the door and said,

"I'm so sorry to have to call you in like this, but I have some bad news. We have intercepted a cable from a new Islamic Group and you Mrs. Brunson, are target for kidnapping within 72 hours at the Salome Traffic Circle in Sin el Fil." [That traffic circle was close to our Sin el Fil Nazarene Church and the Nazarene Evangelical School K-9th grades.]

He continued, "You need to take this seriously. Two years ago, a missionary was warned to leave her area. She refused and three days later, she opened her clinic at 8:00 am and someone shot her three times in the head and killed her. This is serious."

Bob and I looked at each other.

Bob asked, "What do you suggest?"

He asked many questions about our work in Lebanon. I asked, "Can you give us some documentation so we can show our leaders what is going on?"

"No, but I can talk to you leaders."

Bob gave them the phone number of the Eurasia Regional Office in Switzerland. We knew they were in meetings. The attaché called and spoke with Lindell Browning. He explained why we were in danger and the need for our protection to be increased. Lindell got on the phone with Bob.

"Bob, I want you to leave immediately. Do not worry about your personal items. We will see to it that all is taken care of. But you and Norma leave as soon as possible."

Bob had a problem. His passport was in immigration getting his resident visa renewed. Mine was already renewed. It was Friday and during Ramadan. No government offices were open on Friday. The attaché said someone would pick up Bob's passport tomorrow, Friday.

They worked with our travel agent to secure a Lufthansa ticket for me leaving that night at 3:00 am. They also said they would put guards around our apartment. The attaché told said, "Tonight at midnight four men in two cars will come to get you, Mrs. Brunson. They will take you to the airport and will do the same tomorrow night after Mr. Brunson has his passport."

We were in shock. He told us not to tell anyone. But we knew we needed to tell the Director of the School, our close friend, Abdo. We hid our car and walked up the back way to their apartment. We cried and hugged as we knew we would most likely not meet again here on earth. They followed us back to our apartment, we hugged goodbye.

and Bob began sorting our belongings; mission, personal and to sell. I packed all I could.

I was afraid to call my family back in the United States, but knew I had to let them know what was happening. I called my brother Ray and spoke briefly to him in Spanish. I told him I thought our phone was tapped, but in code let him know what was happening.

Our doorbell rang at midnight. Bob answered the intercom. It was my ride. He picked up my suitcases and we rode the elevator down to the 1st floor. We didn't say much. It was quiet and it felt eerie.

We said hello, they took my suitcase. Bob and I hugged each other, and he whispered, "Norma, be strong. God is with us." As I got into the back seat of the front car, and threw Bob kiss and a wave, I asked myself if I was living someone else's nightmare or was it really mine.

We arrived at the airport, and they whisked me through security and immigration with a gun-toting guard by our side. The man that had ridden in the front seat stayed with me until my 3:00 am flight arrived, I boarded, and the door was closed. I still could not believe this was happening.

There was a full moon that night, shinning over the city of Beirut. As the plane took off, I knew I would never be back. I remembered the full moon when God spoke to me about being a missionary. Somehow that night I knew that my time as overseas missionary was ending. My tears fell in sadness and fear. What would the future hold now?

I worried about Bob's safety. I prayed and asked God to protect him. I thought about our friends, who through the turmoil of war, bombings, and instability, must remain, living through the chaos day by day. And Bob and I were able to get out. I felt it was unfair.

My flight landed in Frankfort. I had a long lay over. The seats were so uncomfortable. I was tense. I was stressed. I was afraid for Bob. When I arrived the next day at O'Hair in Chicago, I tried calling Beirut from a public phone, but I discovered one could not call the Middle East from public phones.

I was relieved to finally arrive in Kansas City. I couldn't wait until Bob arrived the next day. I was finally able to hug him safely the following afternoon. We thanked God for His protection and guidance. We thanked God that our government personnel were so helpful and protective of us as its citizens. We were blessed. We lived with Ray and Claire until we moved into the missionary home in Olathe.

BRAND NEW SET OF PLANS

We were told that since we were so close to retirement, they would not re-deploy us, but would allow us to do deputation until we retired. We traveled all over the Unites States speaking in churches, telling the story of how God is working despite the struggles, wars, and uncertainties.

I applied in four states for a Chaplain's position and was hired as full-time chaplain at Mercy Medical Center in Oklahoma City. I began working in June of 2007. We purchased our first home in Bethany. We retired from the Department of World Mission on February 25, 2008, and began attending Bethany First Church of the Nazarene.

CHAPTER XXII

BETHANY LIFE AGAIN

*W*e never dreamed of returning to Bethany to live, but God always has a plan. I had wonderful experiences in dealing with patients at Mercy. I felt God was really using me to reach people at times when they were needy and open to consider God's love for them.

Bob and I had learned so much about each other. We had grown in our love and understanding. We enjoyed out first-time home and found fulfillment in arranging the yard, with plants and flowers. Bob worked hard one spring by planting with compost, 12 tomato plants in our back yard. We were so anticipating eating home-grown tomatoes! To our chagrin, the summer heat of 104 degrees burned the new blooms. They fell off and we had not one tomato that year!

Bob directed the Course of Study in Spanish for those preparing for ministry. He enjoyed woodcarving and building a Carving hut in the backyard. Bob was happy. We had our granddaughter living with us for several years. The day came when she went back to living with her mother.

I enjoyed driving up to Kansas City to visit my mother and Ray and Claire. During these years, my brother Ray Hendrix, died of glioblastoma. It was so hard to see my brother suffer. But he fought to the end. My mother was doing well, but when pneumonia took over, she knew her time was nearing to meet the Lord. She passed away in January 2014 at the age 105. I still miss them both so much.

One day, I met a lady who asked me what I did. I also told her that I was fluent in Spanish. She jumped at that information. "We need you where I work!"

"Where do you work?"

"The FBI. And we need Spanish Linguists. Would you want to apply?"

I started laughing. I thought, well, why not? So, after completing 64 pages of application, two five-hour sessions of polygraph, battery of tests and one-a-half years later, I because a Full-Time Linguist with the FBI. I was headquartered in Oklahoma City but worked a month at a time all over the United States.

That's another book.

BOB'S HEART

One day Bob started moaning and saying he had pain in his chest. I quickly called 911. Bob was having a heart attack. They rushed him the Oklahoma Heart Hospital and after many tests, was told by Dr. Randolph that he needed quadruple by-pass surgery and a valve replacement.

The day was set for surgery in April of 2014. I had my family and church friends praying. Bob came through well.

Because of Bob's health, we both saw the need for me to be home with him. I resigned my position with the FBI in May 2014. Since our house was paid for, we prayed about God's will for us.

CHAPTER XXIII

BRADENTON, FLORIDA

$\mathcal{W}$e knew about the Missionary Village in Bradenton, now called il Villaggio. Our friends reported all the wonderful aspects of living in Florida. Bob and I thought and prayed about it and made a trip to Florida in August of 2014. We fell in love with the weather, the birds, the beauty, and the residents. We prayed about it, sold our home, and moved to Bradenton in December of 2014.

Our first couple of years were filled with the joy of living in the beauty of God's fresh nature. We celebrated our 50th wedding anniversary by taking a 5,000-mile trip up the east coast, through the New England States, visiting friends and enjoying the blessings of sightseeing, boat rides, museum trips and just being together. They were days of joy, relaxation, and enjoyment of one another. I thank God every day for those wonderful days together.

Bob and I had worked through many challenging kinks in our relationship. There was not a couple on earth that was more diverse in temperament and preferences. Bob was a detailist. I am a generalist. Bob was an introvert. I am an extrovert. Bob is an artist. Norma cannot draw. Bob's father was the dominant parent. Norma's mother was the dominant parent. Bob's culture was a California-USA American. Norma's is half Latin American and half USA American cultures.

Bob took his time in making decisions and sometimes delayed too long. Norma makes quick decisions and sometimes makes a mistake. Bob loved western movies. Norma loves comedy ones. Bob liked to play Rook to WIN. Norma likes to play Rook to PLAY.

But what united us was greater than our differences. We both had placed God first in our lives even before we met. We both felt a call to ministry, and especially to peoples who still had not heard the Good News of Salvation through Jesus Christ. We both came from pastor's families. Both of our fathers were brought to faith because of the personal outreach of a layman. Both of our families' history was changed because of that layman.

Bob and I had the same parenting skills [or lack of them!] But we felt that children should be trained in the things of God and disciplined with love and kindness, but firmness and wisdom. Both Bob and I were the middle child. Both Bob and I were Ordained Elders in the Church of the Nazarene.

We both enjoyed signing duets together. We liked football and watched the Chicago Bears or the Kansas City Chiefs with keen interest. We appreciated eating out

together, visiting museums and taking in the sights once we
had leisure time in Florida.

We attended Bradenton First Church of the Nazarene
and made many good friends. I was asked to teach the
Regeneration Sunday School class. What an honor that
was! During the winter months, many Sundays, our class
grew to over 150. God was gracious in giving me the opportunity to serve my Lord and my church in this way.

One day I received a call about a chaplain's position at
Manatee Memorial Hospital in Bradenton. I applied and
got the job. I found it rewarding and a blessing to be able
to be Director of Pastoral Care in such a busy place. God's
love, compassion and call were so evident in patients that I
came to know. It was a joy to serve God in that capacity. I
made lasting friends and I am eternally grateful for all God
allowed me to experience.

It was a supreme joy when I felt God allowed me to lead
a patient to Christ. One day a young man came in and was
on life support. He was not doing well at all. I spoke with
his distraught parents, offering comfort and encouragement.
I could not talk with John, because of his weakened condition. After about two weeks of his hospital stay, I felt led to
approach his bed. He was on life support, eyes closed, as
he had been since arriving. I asked the nurse,

"Has he been awake at all today?"

"No, I don't think so,"

"Well, I'm going to ask him if he would like for me to
offer prayer for him."

I approached the patient, "John, this is chaplain Norma, I wondered, would you like for me to offer prayer for you?"

To my utter surprise, he nodded slightly. The nurse called out, "He said yes!"

I began to pray. I thanked God that He knew John. I thanked God that John was knit beautifully in his mother's womb. I thanked God that Jesus died on the cross for John's sins and for mine. Then I prayed with more gusto,

"John, the thief on the cross didn't do anything except look to Jesus with eyes of love and need. John, look to Jesus today. He is listening to our prayer. Jesus loves you, Lift your heart to Jesus!"

John slowly lifted his head towards the ceiling. The nurse and I gasped. I continued, "Yes, John, look to the saving love of Jesus. He forgives your sins. Confess him as Your Lord. He died to forgive us. Accept His forgiveness right now! You belong to Him!"

John kept his head looking upward. I concluded the prayer. And asked,

"John, are you aware that Jesus really loves you?" His eyes turned up in a faint smile and he gave a slight nod. I shared with his parents and sister. They cried for joy. John died two days later. What a privilege I had to pray with him on that day!

There are many more victories. But that's another book and I already have the title!

BOB NOT WELL

Bob began losing weight. He said he wasn't feeling well much of the time. I noticed that he spent more time in the recliner and had lost interest in going and doing.

The diagnosis came as a shock, "Hodgkin's Lymphoma and Prostate Cancer". Both cancers were ravaging in his body. He underwent chemotherapy but because of the regrowth of the Hodgkin's Lymphoma, he could not tolerate radiation. One day he said, "I feel it's my time to go."

His oncologist recommended a brand-new chemotherapy but warned that it had severe side effects and only 30% live to three years recovery. Bob said, "No, not for me."

He fell seven times in one day. I couldn't lift him and called strong men in the village to help get him up. One day he said he had prayed about it and knew that it was time. He told the doctor that he was refusing chemo and wanted to go on Hospice.

I was stunned. We had prayed that God's will be done. But I wasn't ready for this. We had superb help as we found out all the accommodations that Tidewell Hospice would provide. It was difficult. I wasn't prepared.

BOB IN THE ARMS OF JESUS

Bob's last few months were days of quiet reflection. He talked at length about his walk with the Lord. His daily verse was, "Search me oh God and know my heart; try me and know my anxious thoughts; and see if there be any wicked way in me and lead in the way everlasting." [Psalm 139:23]

He was transferred to the Sarasota Hospice House. Sheri and her son Aison came to be with Bob and me during his last days. Sheri was an incredible tower of strength for me during those weeks. Bob's sister Nancy Cauthron and grandson Nate Davis came to tell Bob goodbye. Many friends visited Bob. We had beautiful times of prayer and praise, even as I knew his time was short.

Robin was in the air, flying from Argentina when Bob died at 4:27 am on October 29, 2018. It was also Sheri's birthday.

We held two memorial services: one in Bradenton, Florida and the other in Bethany, Oklahoma. Bob's remains are buried in Oklahoma City.

CHAPTER XXIV

BECOMING A WIDOW

*I*t takes time to realize that everything changes when one's husband of 54 years is gone. It took me and is still taking "mental and emotional adjustment" to this new role. I am incredibly grateful that Robin was able to be with me for a month following our service in Bethany. She and Sheri both were a great comfort to me.

However, my life had entered a new phase. I noticed that my pace was quicker at the hospital. I did not want to linger long in the face of suffering. Suddenly I was not as comfortable with death, especially when couples lost a spouse. I walked out from offering ministry on two occasions, because my personal grief was overwhelming.

I worked hard and answered the midnight on-calls. I was busy but I felt I was not serving to the best of my capacity. Half of me was gone.

BATTLING THE WINDS

Outside the wind is howling,
A storm in on the way,
Palm trees grip the ground for comfort,
Debris is flying everywhere.

They promised it'd be raining.
But would not last for long,
So, as the wind screams loud and full,
I'm sheltered in my home.

But then my home is empty,
My husband's gone for sure.
And while the hours gently roll,
I feel his absence more.

I wonder how one copes real well,
When part of one is gone away,
How does one simply journey on?
When storms abate one's soul?

I do not like the howling wind,
I do not like the storms, the rains,
I do not like the times alone
That compete with winds at night.

I have no answer in this prose,
There's no solution to depose,
I fear I must just travel on,
And deal with pain, and just be strong.

And when I feel I must recant,
I'll hold on closer to His Hand.
And though I do not understand,
I'll follow Him through storms and sand.
Norma Brunson 2/6/2020

My friend Libbie and I decided to take a trip to Kentucky and experience The Ark. I wanted to get away. She made the arrangements, and I pulled the attic ladder down to climb up and get my suitcase.

It was Sunday, August 4, 2019, at 4:00 pm. I had no problem with just popping up there and bouncing on down. Except this day, the suitcase decided to take a dive. In attempting to retrieve it, I fell from the 5th rung and landed on my right leg onto the tile floor. I was alone.

CHAPTER XXV

BUSTED TIBIAL PLATEAU

*T*he pain was unbearable. I was screaming in agony. I could hardly breathe. I feared fainting, but I knew I needed help. Where was my phone!

"Oh God, help!" Somehow, I dragged myself into the living room. There right on the table was my phone. I called two friends and they were unavailable. I was finally able to get Adele. She was so comforting. But my screams and the sirens alarmed my neighbors. I knew I had broken something. The leg was swelling fast.

In the middle of my most excruciating pain, I suddenly envisioned Jesus on the cross in great physical pain. Out of the depths of my soul I started thanking Jesus for all He did on the cross for me. "Oh Jesus, how did you stand the physical pain! On top of the separation from the Father, and the sins of the world on you, how did you do it? Thank you, Jesus, for what you did for me!" Screams and more screams!

The ambulance ride was horrendous, but the EMT was kind and patient, helping me as I cried more pain tears that I knew I had.

The ambulance pulled into Manatee Memorial Hospital, where I was Director of Pastoral Care. The help was amazing. The pain agonizing. I went into surgery and had two external poles drilled into my legs to keep my leg straight until the swelling diminished. The doctor said, "You really did a number on your leg. Your tibial plateau is shattered into more pieces than we can count. We quit counting at six!"

The next two days faded into a blurred memory: terrible pain, unbearable misery, kind and thoughtful visitors, and loving care from staff and friends alike. Every move of my body elicited pain. I was helpless as never before.

I was moved to rehab to wait for my second surgery. I cannot explain those days accurately, but several times I told Libbie I just wanted to go to heaven. My pain was too much.

One of my most humbling experiences was the first time I needed to use the bed pan. To get my hips onto the bed pan, I had to push up with my good leg, but in so doing, the broken leg screamed with pain. The rods kept the leg together, but when I moved hips or the other leg, inwardly those broken pieces of bone moved. I can't describe the pain.

Finally, I mustered all the strength I had left and lifted my hips onto the pan. There I was, awkwardly lying on a bed pan. The kind nurse left me alone and said, "Just push your call button when you are done."

That was half of the battle. But I'll leave it to your imagination. Having finished the procedure, I knew the second
most humiliating part of this process would test my self-
pride. Someone had to wipe my bottom. I pushed the call
button and said a prayer, "Oh God, how humiliating!"

She came in and all I could say was, "I'm so sorry you
have to do this!" She looked at me and said, "Honey, this
is my job and I do it gladly 'cause someday I will have to
have someone help me!" I surrendered to the humiliation
and learned a great lesson.

I had said "NO!" several times in my life: at the age of
three when I misbehaved in church. I said "NO!" at the age
of 12 when I decided to take my punishment standing up. I
said "NO!", at the age of 40 when I said "NO" to giving in to
depression and despair and walked into a Psyche Ward. I said
"NO", to depression when Bob died. There was a constant,
"No, I will not lie down, I'll take this standing up, thank you!"

But now, I could stand no longer. Certainly, not physically, but now internally. I had to surrender to my weakness,
my inability to care for myself, my utter dependence on
others to feed, clothe, and bathe me and care for my most
personal needs. I had come to an end to standing. What
was I to learn?

BOWERS, LIBBIE

Libbie Bowers became an angel in my life. She lived in
il Villaggio. Libbie is five years older than I. She had been a

Social Worker and taught Social Work at Eastern Nazarene College in Boston, MA. Libbie became the person that took care of bringing me mail, washing my clothes, helping with banking, sitting with me, listening to me moan and groan. Libbie was incredible.

I will never understand how she withstood the hours and days of visiting me in the first rehab and then the second rehab following my second surgery. She was an angel God provided for me. Bob had been gone 10 months. I missed him so much at this time, but Libbie became a friend indeed. I do not know how I would have made it without her. God knew and He supplied. Libbie picked up the responsibility of helping me until I was weight bearing.

No orthopedic surgeon in two major hospitals would tackle my leg. A trauma orthopedic surgeon from Florida Orthopedic finally accepted to perform surgery on my leg. I was glad when I knew they would finally take the external rods off my legs. My second surgery was performed on August 14. It took four hours. My surgeon said, "You have two plates and 13 screws in your leg." You really messed up your leg. You have changed your life forever."

He had no idea how targeted his statement was.

BUSTED LEG

I had two legs that walked for miles,
They stood the test, they even smiled,
I had two knees that bent at will.
And then at night they rested still.
I had two feet that never quit.
They stretched and moved, climbed every hill.

So, I was fine, and life was good.
And all marched well as I knew it should.
But then one day to my surprise
The ladder moved, or so I'll say,
And down I came with a crashing sway,
To shatter the bones in my leg that day.

The pain was great, the screams were greater,
The neighbors came to help gain shelter.
And then a journey did begin
Of hurt, of strain, of stress and pain.
I never dreamed my life would crash,
With such a bang, with such a smash.

The rehab folk were sweet and kind.
And made me work and made me climb.
The steps of growth, of muscle gain
Until the day their words were plain:
"You now can leave. We wish you well,
Work hard you must. You've just been swell."

It's been three months since that fateful day,
In poem's form I have much to say,
Today I walked with a brand-new friend,
The walker-yes – left the chair behind.
With grin and grit, I knew it was time.
To stretch this brand-new leg of mine.

What have I learned through these past days?
Some I will share, some I will not.
But all in all, this thing I know,
That God is good He does not fail.
That friends are many who will help the frail.
I learned I make it with grit and strength.
Supplied by God, my life journey's length.

I'm learning now to climb again,
The ladder of silence, trust, and rest
And knowing that as I climb this hill,
I'll fall on Him, His Grace, His Will.
Norma Brunson, November 4, 2019

I resigned my position at Manatee Memorial Hospital. I knew it was a long journey to recovery. It was hard to say good-bye to personnel that had become good friends. A wonderful young man has taken that position and is just the man for the hour.

I lost my husband. I suffered a major break to my tibial plateau and was incapacitated for five months. I lost my job. All these plus more traumas came to me at once. I had days of deep sorrow. Days of pain and great discomfort. I was in a huge hole many days during these months.

But what friends I had. So many kindnesses poured out on me. I was truly blessed.

I took a day to pray and fast. God knew I needed it. I was fragmented, tense, alone, confused. I started the day reading from God Calling,

"Your Red Sea. Go forward fearlessly. Do not think about the Red Sea that lies ahead. Be very sure that when you come to it the waters will part and you will pass over to your promised land of freedom."

Thank you, Jesus. I closed my door and went into my Prayer Room. God was near. Several passages blessed me. "Though my mother and father leave me, God will gather me in."

"All my fountains are in you."

I was praying when I saw myself in the middle of the Pacific Ocean. I was not drowning. I wore a life jacket. It was a sunny day, but I was not hot. I was just floating alone. I felt alone. Terribly alone. I called out to Jesus.

Suddenly I saw him in the distance walking on the water towards me. He was tall and strong. I was small. He came to me and smiled, and I said, "Please help me. I'm so alone out here!" He picked me up and walked all the way on the water to a wide and beautiful beach. I was dripping wet. He gently set me down. I asked him, "Where are you going to take me? Where will I land?"

He said, "For now I want you to enjoy the beach. Just play on the sand. We will go inland later. For now, chase the sea gulls, find seashells, build sandcastles, lie down, and watch the clouds. I will be here with you and watch over you so that you do not wander away and you are safe. Feel free to go play on the beach for a while."

I tried to wander off the beach, but I noticed that he did not follow. And I certainly did to want to be anywhere without him. So, I played. I showed him a seashell and he said, "I created it's mother and father a long time ago. I am glad you found it!" I felt joy and freedom. I was not alone. I also realized that I ran without pain, and I jumped around without hesitation. It brought joy to my soul to know that He, my Lord, my Husband, my Master, and my Friend would be with me, no matter what.

As I pen these words it is nearing two and a half years since Bob's death and two years since my fall. It takes grit to face and overcome depression and selfish pity. But it is God's Grace that stocks the soul with fortitude and sustaining power.

Grit and Grace, hand in hand. And God supplies them both.

CPSIA information can be obtained
at www.ICGtesting.com
Printed in the USA
BVHW040347280322
632494BV00001B/3